ewart Aiken, Rafael Alarcon, N. Aldridge, Ron Aleks, Skip Alexander, Steven Alker, Don Allan, Steve Allan, Fulton Allem, Michael Allen, Johnny Allen, Ras Allen, Robert Allenby, Bud
son, J.C. Anderson, Jerry Anderson, Rob Anderson, Steve Anderson-Chapman, Billy Andrade, Dale Andreason, Jason Andrew, A.H. Anger, Fred Annon, David Anthony. Isao Aoki, Stuart
old, Perry Arthur, Howard Atkinson, C. Attridge, Emlyn Aubrey, A.E. Austin, Woody Austin, Tom Aycock, Alex Ayton, George Ayton, Laurie Ayton, Paul Azinger, Aaron Baddeley, Briny
Barber, Jerry Barber, Miller Barber, Craig Barlow, B. Barnabe, Michael Barnblatt, Jim M. Barnes, Rob Barnet, Rob Barnett, Dave Barr, Ray Barr Jr., Todd Barranger, ... rett, W.
eg Baxter, George Bayer, C.H. Beamish, Andy Bean, Frank Beard, Ballard Beasley, Bob Beauchemin, Yvan Beauchemin, J.A. Beaupre, C ... Notah
anio Jr., Bill Bergin, George Bernadin, Lindsay Bernakevitch, John Berry, Shane Bertsch, Scott Bess, Al Besselink, Mickey Bessignano, ... , Roy
Black, Ronnie Black, Mike Blackburn, Woody Blackburn, Phil Blackmar, H.C. Blair, J.C. Blair, James Blair, Jay Don Blake, Homero Blan ... quist,
Bonse, Eric Booker, Aubrey Boomer, Ernest Boros, Ernie Boros, Guy Boros, Jim Boros, Julius Boros, Hugh Borthwick, Dick Borthwick, ... , Bob
ichael Brannan, Bill Brask, Alan Bratton, Oscar Brault, Roland Brault, W.F. Brazier, W.T. Brazier, Bobby Breen, Jeff Brehaut, Kevin Br ... ckley,
Fred Brown, Jack R. Brown, Ken Brown, Louis Brown, Matt Brown, Pete Brown, R.F. Brown, William Brown, Olin Browne, Phil Brow ... , Bart
Burke, Bob Burns, George Burns, Gordon Burns , Jock Burns, Robert Burns, Clark Burroughs, Kevin Burton, Dick Bury, Hal Butler, Bla ... man,
ell, A.V. Campbell, Joe Campbell, Larry Campbell, Fred Canausa, David Canipe, Billy Capps, Howard Capps, Joe Cardenas, Sam Carmichae ... , Mark Carnevale, Jason Caron,
Chain, Greg Chalmers, Brandel Chamblee, Jim Chancey, Mark Chapleski, Bob Charles, Barry Cheesman, T.C. Chen, Don Cherry, Lee Chill, L. Chiappette, Bill Chinery, Clair Chinery,
pett, Bobby Clark, Jimmy Clark, K.D. Clark, Michael Clark II, Tim Clark, Paul Claxton, J. H. Clay, Dave Clayton, F. C. Clayton, Keith Clearwater, Lennie Clements, Jose Coceres, Russ
Compston, Erik Compton, W.P. Compton, Byron Comstock, Charles W. Congdon, Tim Conley, Frank Conner, Jack Conrad, Joe Conrad, Charles Coody, Jeff Cook, John Cook, John Cook,
n, Gene Counter, Fred Couples, Charles Courtney, Gary Cowan, Mark Coward, Bob Cox, Wiffy L. Cox, Rick Cramer, Bruce Crampton, Lyle Crawford, Richard Crawford, Tom Creavy,
umming, Lou Cumming, W.S. Cumming, Michael Cunning, Robert Cunningham, Bob Cunningham Jr., Reg Cunningham, W. Cunningham, W.T. Cunningham, Bobby Joe Cupit, Buster
ly, Mike Daly, Doug Dalziel, Patrick Damron, Robert Damron, George Daniel, George Daniels, Mike David, W. David, Ken Davidson, Steven Davies, Dave Davis, Ed Davis, John Davis,
elsing, Jimmy Demaret, Constant Demattia, Rolf Deming, Todd Demsey, Clark Dennis, Jim Dent, Jerry De Sio, A.D. Desjardins, Arthur Desjardins, Joe Devaney, Paul Devenport, Dave
Dion, Dave Dixon, John Doctor, Steve Doctor, Trevor Dodds, Leonard Dodson, Don Doe, Arthur Doering, Jay Dolan, Jim Dolan, Luke Donald, Mike Donald, Todd Doohan, Ed Dougherty,
udley, Ken Duggan, Ken Duke, Doug Dunakey, Skip Dunaway, J. Duncan, G.M. Duncan, Gordon Duncan Jr., Bill Dunk, Bill Dunn, Bobby Dunn, Joe Durant, Mortie Dutra, Olin Dutra,
ve Eichelberger, Steve Eichelberger, Steve Eichstaedt, H. Eidsvig, Brad Elder, George Elder, George Elder, Lee Elder, Ockie Eliason, Steve Elkington, John Elliott, Danny Ellis, J.F. Ellis,
vans, Max Evans, Tom Evans, Tony Evans, H.W. Eve, Jack Ewing, Joe Ezar, William Ezinicki , Keith Eynon, Brad Fabel, Alan Fadel, Nick Faldo, Don Fairfield, Elwin Fanning, Todd
Ferguson, Cec Ferguson, D.A. Ferguson, Dave Ferguson, Jim Ferree, Gene Ferrell, James Ferriell, Jim Ferrier, Mike Fetchick, Forrest Fezler, Rudy Fieltz, T. Filmore, Allan Findlay, P.R.
ty Fleckman, Bruce Fleisher, Pete Fleming, Steve Flesch, H.C. Fletcher, Pat Fletcher, Gary Floan, Ray Floyd, H.S. Foley, Ron Folk, Ken Folkes, Tommy Fonseca, A.V. Ford, Bobby Ford,
Alex Fraser, C.C. Fraser, Howell Fraser, Scotty Fraser, Frank P. Freeman, Ray Freeman, Robin Freeman, William M. Freeman, Emmett French, Bob Friend, David Frost, S. Fry, Edward
m Gallagher Jr., Bill Galloway, Jack Galloway, Alex Galt, Robert Gamez, Stephen Gangluff, H. Gans, Ivan Gantz, Sergio Garcia, Buddy Gardner, Tom Garner, Bill Garrett, Andy Gaspar,
Gibby Gilbert, Bob Gilder, A.G. Gill, Derek Gillespie, G.J. Gillespie Jr., Ron Gillespie, Walter Gilliam, Tom Gillis, Roger Ginsberg, Ken Girard, F. Girmonde, Marc Girouard, Phil Giroux,
in, Ted Goin, John Golden, Joel Goldstrand, Jaime Gomez, Ernie Gonzalez, Jaime Gonzalez, Lan Gooch, Jimmie Good, A.L. Gooderham, Danny Goodman, R.B. Goodwin, W. Goodwin,
ady, David Graham, Lou Graham, F.T. Grant, Jim Grant, W.C. Grant, Glenn Gray, Thomas Gray, R.M. Gray Jr., Robert T. Gray, D. Green, Eric Green, Hubert Green, Jimmy Green, Ken
Gary Groh, John Gross, Kelly Grunewald, Charles Guest, Ralph Guldahl, L. Gullickson, Joey Gullion, Scott Gump, Graham Gunn, John Gustin, Ted Gwin, Fred Haas Jr., Hunter Haas,
Halpern, Arthur Ham, John Hamarik, Gar Hamilton, Stu Hamilton, Laurie Hammer, Donnie Hammond, Mike Hammond, Harry Hampton, Phil Hancock, S. Hancock, Dick Hanscom,
ton, Labron Harris Jr., Michael Harris, Bob Harrison, E.J. Harrison, Dudley Hart, Jeff Hart, Steve Hart, Len Harvey, Barry Harwell, R. Hastings, Morris Hatalsky, Jerry Hatfield, Fred
Hebert, Marion Heck, Wes Heffernan, Harry Hei, Mike Heinen, Bob Heintz, Webb Heintzelman, G.B. Heintzman, Roy Heisler, Stuart Hendley, Mark Henderson, R. Henderson, Peter
ler, Eduardo Herrera, A.W. Heron, Tim Herron, John Heslop, Bruce Heuchan, Jeff Hewes, Greg Hickman, Satoshi Higashi, Mike Higgins, Peter Hildrop, Dave Hill, Guy Hill, Jason Hill,
Hoch, W. M. Hodgson, Bud Hofmeister, Ben Hogan, Eddie Hogan, James Hogan, Richard Holden, Dick Holden, Mike Holland, Tony Hollifield, Bud Holscher, Bill Holt, Herb Holzscheiter,
harles Howell III, Dick Howell, Ryan Howison, Bradley Hughes, James Huish, Arthur J. Hulbert, Mike Hulbert, Ed Humenik, A. Hunt, Fred Hunt, Norman Hunt, Fred Hunter, James
Hutchison, Ralph Hutchison, Ian Hutchings, Brian Hutton, G.A. Hutton, Hugh Inggs, Stu Ingraham, Bob Inman, Joe Inman, John Inman, Walker Inman Jr., E.A. Innes, John Innes, Hale
Jamieson, Jim Jamieson, Don January, Lee Janzen, Hugh Jacques, Norm Jarvis, S. Jawer, Tommy Jenkins, Tom Jenkins, Lorne Jennex, Jim Jewell, David Jiminez, Brandt Jobe, Per-Ulrik
ob Johnson, Al Johnston, Bill Johnston, Jimmy Johnston, John Johnston, Ralph Johnston, W. Johnston, James Johnstone, Philip Jonas, C.M. Jones, D.A. Jones, Gene Jones, Gordon Jones,
Kane, Yoshinori Kaneko, Robert Karlsson, Hideki Kase, Monty Kaser, Ricky Kawagishi, Walt Kawakami, Andrew Kay, B. Kay, Jack Kay, Jack Kay Jr., Jonathan Kaye, Dan Keefe, Arthur
l Kennedy, Daniel Kenny, John Kenny, Rick Keown, Ben Kern, Fred Kern Jr., Paul Kern, Ben Kerr, Bill Kerr, Sam Kerr, Tom Kerrigan, Stanley Kertes, Gerry Kesselring, Darrell Kestner,
Kite, Bob Kivlin, Roger Klatt, Chuck Klein, Jeff Klein, Willie Klein, Kent Kluba, Scott Knapp, Harold Kneece, Dick Knight, John Knight, Arden Knoll, Kenny Knox, George Knudson,
M. Kreiger, Cliff Kresge, Ed Kringle, Ted Kroll, Gary Krueger, Kenichi Kuboya, Hank Kuehne, Matt Kuchar, Gene Kunes, Charles Lacey, Huston LaClair, Greg Ladehoff, Ky Laffoon,
rt, John Langford, Franklin Langham, Jim Langley, Jeffrey Lankford, Brad Lardon, Gene Larkin, Gilles Larochelle, Wilfred Larseingue, Duff Lawrence, Palmer Lawrence, Peter Laws,
onard, James Lepp, Greg Lesher, Perry Leslie, Ron Letellier, Gavin Levenson, Dave Levesque, Thomas Levet, Wayne Levi, Don Levin, John Levinson, Bud Lewis, J.L. Lewis, Jack Lewis,
Lawson Little, W. Little, Gene Littler, Jack Littler, Bill Lively, John Lively, David Llewellyn, Charles Lock , Willie F. Lock, Willie J. Lock, Bobby Locke, Frank E. Locke, P.E. Locke, Bud
Steve Lowery, Buck Luce, David Lundstrom, Bob Lunn, Buddy Lutz, Mark Lye, Keith Lyford, R. Lyle, Sandy Lyle, A. Lynch, F. Lyon, George S. Lyon, Seymour Lyon, Dick Lytle, J.E.
nes, John Mahaffey, Hunter Mahan, Mac Main, Robert Mair, Peter Major, Ted Makalena, Roger Maltbie, J. Malutic, Larry Mancour, Tony Manero, Mark Maness, Lloyd Mangrum, Ray
itz R. Martin, George Martin, Iverson Martin, J. Martin, James C. Martin, W. Martin, Wes Martin, Bill Martindale, Richard Martinez, Milon Marusic, Shigeki Maruyama, Bunny Mason,
Billy Maxwell, Bob May, Dick Mayer, Billy Mayfair, Shelley Mayfield, Joe Mazziotti, A.W.G. McAllister, Walter McAlpine, R.J. McAulliffe, Rives McBee, J. McBride, Blaine McCallister,
on, Wayne McDonald, Graeme McDowell, R.A. McDougall, Walter McElroy, Jerry McGee, Mike McGee, Tom McGinnis, John McGough, Jim McGovern, J.G. McGowan, Jack McGowan,
ndrew McLardy, A. McLean, George McLean, D.V. McLean, B.R. "Mac" McLendon, Peter McLeod, W. McLuckie, Rob McMillan, John McMullin, T. McNamara, Artie McNickle, E.J.
eister, Al Mengert, Adam Mednick, Steve Melnyk, Bob Menne, Sonny Methvin, Dick Metz, Micheal Mezei, Chico Miartuz, John Micallef, Louis Michaud, Shaun Micheel, Phil Mickelson,
Lindy Miller, Massie B. Miller, Honald Millett, Jon Mills, Bobby Mitchell, Jeff Mitchell, Mike Mitchell, R. Mitchell, W.G. Mitchell, Katsumasa Miyamoto, Larry Mize, Kris Moe, Mahlon
. Moonsaty, Joe Moore, Ossie Moore, Parker Moore, Richard L. Moore, Tommy Moore, Paul Moran, Bob Moreland, Gil Morgan, J. Morgan, John E. Morgan, S. Morgan, David Morland
n Muirhead, W.H. Mulligan, W. Mulligan, Rod Munday, Allan Mundle, W.L. Munn, J. Munro, Frank Murchie, Bill Murchison, Bob Murphy, Sean Murphy, Albert H. Murray, Charles R.
Newman, Dave Newquist, Jack Newton, S.H. Newton, S.M. Newton, Bobby Nichols, Gil Nichols, Jack Nicklaus, Gary Nicklaus, Jack W. Nicklaus II, J.W. Nicol, Mike Nicolette, Lonnie
Vern Novak, Rod Nuckolls, Aaron Oberholser, Michael O'Conner, Pat O'Donnell, Alvin Odom, W. Ogg , Joe Ogilvie, Geoff Ogilvy, Brett Ogle, Mac O'Grady, Leo O'Grady, David Ogrin,
i Ono, Peter Oosterhuis, Steve Oppermann, George Ormiston, Gary Ostrega, Jay Overton, Roy Pace, Gareth Paddison, Harold D. Paddock, Don Padgett, Anthony Painter, Arnold Palmer,
Parks Jr., Jesper Parnevik, Craig Parry, Jerry Pate, Steve Pate, L. Patenaude, Hugh Paterson, Ron Paterson, Wilson Paterson, J.M. Patterson, Chris Patton, J.M. Patton, G.D. Paulson, Carl
est Penfold, Tony Penna, Jack Penrose, David Peoples, Pat Perez, Jean-Guy Periard, Ray Periard, C.H. Perkins, Phil Perkins, Craig Perks, Tom Pernice Jr., Mike Pero, L. Perriard, Chris
Bobby Pinnell, Gary Pinns, M. Pinsonnault, Gary Pitchford, Jerry Pittman, Julius Platte, Gary Player, Wayne Player, Bob Plommer, Dan Pohl, Art Pomy, Don Pooley, Bill Porter, Joe Porter,
Pruitt, Roane Puett, Tom Purdy, Tom Purtzer, Mike Putnam, Leo K. Quesnel, Smiley Quick, Brett Quigley, Dana Quigley, Jeff Quinney, Fran Quinn, Sammy Rachels, Dave Ragan, R.M.
on Reese, Edward Reevey, Dean Refram, Victor Regalado, H.S. Reid, Mike Reid, Steve Reid, Wilfrid Reid, Ronnie Reif, Bobby Reith, T.B. Reith, John Restino, Jack Reynolds, Jim Rheim,
my Rimmer, Larry Rinker, Lee Rinker, Steve Rintoul, H.S. Risebrow, Darren Ritchie, Alberto Rivadeneira, Doug Robb, Jack Roberts, Loren Roberts, Alex Robertson, Bruce Robertson,
riguez, Mel Rogers, Guy Rolland, John Rollins, Eduardo Romero, C.C. Ronalds, Bob Rosburg, Bob Rose, Clarence Rose, A.H. Ross, John Ross, Lionel Ross, J. Roswell, Chuck Rotar, Bob
y Rusnak, Jim Rutledge, Arthur S. Russell, Jim Russell, John Russell, F.R. Ryan, L.E. Ryan, Charlie Rymer, Rory Sabbatini, Ed Sabo, Akio Sadakata, Frank Sadler, Harold Salvador, Bill
Marty Schiene, John Schlee, Butch Schlicht, George Schneiter, Paul J. Schodeller, Bob Schoener, Willie Scholl, Dave Schreyer, John Schroeder, Mike Schuchart, Ted Schulz, Pat Schwab,
t Severson, G.S. Seymour, Alf Shand, T. Shannon, Bob Shave, Bob Shave Jr., Bob Shaw, G.P. Shaw, Mickey Shaw, Tom Shaw, Bob Shearer, Patrick Sheehan, Jack Shields, Jr. Shirey, Kerry
g, Gaylon Simon, Jim Simons, Scott Simpson, Tim Simpson, Alfred Sims, A.K. Sinclair, F.K. Sinclair, R. Sinclair, Joey Sindelar, Vijay Singh, Geoffrey Sisk, J.M. Skead, A. Skinner, J.D.
Harold Smith, Horton Smith, Ivan Smith, Jerry Smith, Macdonald Smith, Mike Smith, Neale Smith, Norman Smith, R.C. Smith, Stuart Smith, Taylor Smith, Tom Smith, Warren Smith,
, G. Southam, Craig A. Spence, R.B. Spence, Joel Spinola, David A. Spittal, Willie Spittal, Glenn Spivey, Orest Spooner, Mike Sposa, Jack Spradlin, Steve Spray, Jerry Springer, Marshall
n, W. Iain Steel, Jerry Steelsmith, Joe Steiger, F.R. Steller, F.C. Stephens, Johnny Stevens, N. Stevens, Douglas S. Stewart, Earl Stewart Jr., Payne Stewart, Ray Stewart, T. Stewart, Darron
Straub, Ron Streck, Pinky Stevenson, Steve Stricker, Bobby Stroble, Mark Stuart, Buddy Sullivan, Chip Sullivan, Dennis Sullivan, Joseph A. Sullivan, Mike Sullivan, Rob Sullivan, Vince
ren Sye, Joe Tachan, R. Tait, Daniel Talbot, Stephane Talbot, Dale Tallon, Hidemichi Tanaka, Alan Tapie, Malcolm Tapp, Ken Tarling, Mike Tartaglia, Phil Tataurangi, Ernie Tate, Gordon
erge Thivierge, Dick Thomas, Ron Thomas, Steve Thomas, Alvie Thompson, Barney Thompson, Bill Thompson, Dicky Thompson, Frank Thompson, Jimmy Thompson, Joe Thompson,
nsen, Jimmy Thomson, Peter Thomson, John Thoren, H. Towlson, Ken Towns, David Thore, Chuck Thorpe, Jim Thorpe, Bert Ticehurst, Chris Tidland, Bill Tindall, P.C. Tidy, Dennis
emblay, Yves Tremblay, Lee Trevino, Kirk Triplett, Paul Trittler, Gary Trivisonno, Dennis Trixler, Bill Trombley, W.H. Trovinger, Ken Trowbridge, Alain Trudeau, Mike Tschetter, Chris
H.A. Tyron, Wally Ulrich, L. Ulyers, Hal Underwood, Brett Upper, Omar Uresti, Stan Utley, Bo Van Pelt, Tommy Valentine, Bruce Vaughan, Kenneth Vaughan, Vance Veazey, Ken Venturi,
Wadsworth, Bob Wagner, Grant Waite, Bill Wakeham, Ernie Wakelam, Rocky Walcher, Duffy Waldorf, Cyril Walker, Gil Walker, T.H. Walker, Art Wall Jr., D.B. Walters, Retief Waltman,
n, Tom Watson, F.E. Wattles, Brian Watts, Bill Webb, Ron Weber, Bert Weaver, Billy Weaver, Buddy Weaver, Dewitt Weaver, Doug Weaver, Boo Weekley, D.A. Weibring, Mike Weir, Tom
rton, Dick Whetzle, Frank Whibley, Greg Whisman, Buck White, Carlton White, L.H. White, Larry White, Mike White, Michael Whitney, Don Whitt, Ron Whittaker, Hal Whittingdon,
on, Jeff Wilson, Jim Wilson, John Wilson, Mark Wilson, Bo Wininger, Terry Winter, Larry Wise, Jimmy Wittenberg, Bob Wolcott, Randy Wolff, C.R. Wood, Craig Wood, J. Douglas Wood,
n, Virgil Worsham, Robert Wrenn, Bill Wright, Jim Wright, Tom Wulff, Mark Wurtz, Robert Wylie, Bob Wynn, Mike Wynn, Dudley Wysong, Bert Yancey, Cameron Yancey, Wayne Yates,
Robert J. Zbikowski, Bob Zellie, Walt Zembriski, Bob Zender, John Zibnack, Larry Ziegler, Al Zimmerman, Bob Zimmerman, Billy Ziobro, Fuzzy Zoeller, Richard Zokol

THE OPEN
GOLF CHAMPIONSHIP
OF CANADA

1904–2004

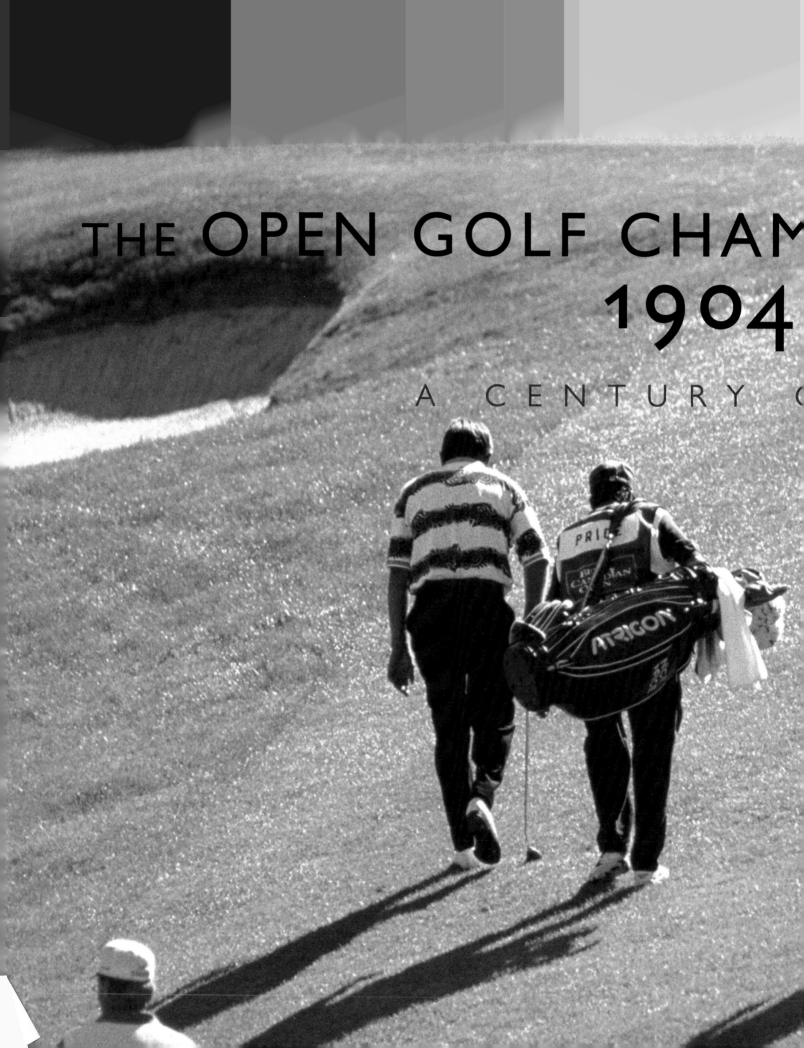

THE OPEN GOLF CHAM
1904

A CENTURY O

PIONSHIP OF CANADA
2004

CHAMPIONS

Edited by KAREN HEWSON
Introduction by IAN CRUICKSHANK

KEY PORTER BOOKS

NATIONAL LIBRARY OF CANADA CATALOGUING IN PUBLICATION

A century of champions : the Open Golf Championship of Canada, 1904–2004 / edited by Karen Hewson.

Includes index.
ISBN 1-55263-562-7

1. Canadian Open Golf Championship—History I. Hewson, Karen

GV970.3.C35C45 2004   796.352'66   C2003-906024-1

THE CANADA COUNCIL | LE CONSEIL DES ARTS
FOR THE ARTS | DU CANADA
SINCE 1957 | DEPUIS 1957

ONTARIO ARTS COUNCIL
CONSEIL DES ARTS DE L'ONTARIO

The publisher gratefully acknowledges the support of the Canada Council for the Arts and the Ontario Arts Council for its publishing program. We acknowledge the support of the Government of Ontario through the Ontario Media Development Corporation's Ontario Book Initiative.

We acknowledge the financial support of the Government of Canada through the Book Publishing Industry Development Program (BPIDP) for our publishing activities.

Key Porter Books Limited
70 The Esplanade
Toronto, Ontario
Canada M5E 1R2
www.keyporter.com

Cover and interior design: Ingrid Paulson

Printed and bound in Canada

04 05 06 07 08 09 6 5 4 3 2 1

PHOTO CREDITS

Allen McInnis, RCGA Collection, 42, 43, 43
Bernard Brault, RCGA Collection, 30, 31, 40, 41, 83, 161, 201, 74, 199, 200
Don Vickery RCGA /du Maurier Collection, 8, 10, 29, 195, 196, 197, 198, 199, 128, 155, 156, 157, 158, 191, 120, 131, 176, 25, 134, 135, 136, 139, 142, 149, 150, 151, 176, 25, 127, 17, 19, 38, 39. 189, 192, 123, 190, 191, 192, 193, 98, 99
Gilbert A. Milne & Co. Toronto, RCGA Collection, 129
Hamilton Golf & Country Club, 94, 95, 96, 97
Henry Koro, 188
Hilles Pickens Collection, RCGA Collection, 56, 182, 122, 183, 16, 84, 114, 118, 119, 185, 181, 184, 185, 186, 113, 115, 66, 70, 37
Lambton Golf & Country Club, 70, 72
MacGreagor Advisory Staff Photos, RCGA Collection, 177, 183,
Michael Burns, (Toronto) RCGA Collection, 190
Michael Fox, RCGA Collection, Ottawa Hunt & Country Club, 189
The Royal Montreal Golf Club, 32, 35
Rosedale Golf Club, 75, 169, 172, 80
Rusty Jarrett—PGA Tour, 198, 194, 196
Shaughnessy Golf & Country Club, 106
Sidney Harris, RCGA Collection, 117
The Globe and Mail, 116
Toronto Golf Club, 44, 48
Toronto Star, 9, 125

All other photographs are from the RCGA Archives, various collections.

Table of Contents

CHAPTER ONE   OPEN GLORY

A Century of Canadian Opens   *Ian Cruickshank* 6

CHAPTER TWO   THE HOST CLUBS

The Royal Montreal Golf Club   *Randy Phillips* 33

Toronto Golf Club   *Karen Hewson* 45

Greater Ottawa   *The Canadian Golfer* 51

Greater Montreal   *Mario Brisebois* 57

Lambton Golf & Country Club   *Ian Cruickshank* 71

Greater Toronto   *John Gordon* 75

Scarboro Golf & Country Club   *Dave Perkins* 85

Riverside Country Club   *Peter McGuire* 91

Hamilton Golf & Country Club   *Garry McKay* 95

Mississaugua Golf & Country Club   *Ian Hutchinson* 101

British Columbia   *Brad Ziemer* 107

Royal York/St. George's   *James Barclay* 113

The Prairies   *Tim Campbell* 119

Southwestern Ontario   *Rick Young* 123

Glen Abbey Golf Club   *Lorne Rubenstein* 129

CHAPTER THREE   THE CHAMPIONS 163

CHAPTER FOUR   THE PRIZE 203

CHAPTER FIVE   THE VOLUNTEERS 209

CHAPTER SIX   THE MEDIA AND THE OPEN 213

CHAPTER SEVEN   RECORDS

Canadian Open Championship 216

Canadian Open 218

INDEX 220

Open Glory

by IAN CRUICKSHANK

A CENTURY *of* CANADIAN OPENS

A century ago, golf was on the cusp of major changes. Hickory sticks and handmade balls still supplied the game's basics in the early 1900s. Professionals were rare, and as yet servants of the golf clubs where they worked, unable even to walk through the front door of the clubhouse. And there were only a few important tournaments: first the British Open, then the U.S. Open and, in 1904, the Canadian Open.

As the game grew, so did the Canadian Open. Over the 100 years it's been played, it has produced some of golf's most memorable moments and hosted its greatest players. Even an abbreviated all-time Canadian Open field includes Bobby Jones, Tommy Armour, Ben Hogan, Walter Hagen, Byron Nelson, Sam Snead, Arnold Palmer, Jack Nicklaus, Tom Watson, Seve Ballesteros, Nick Faldo, Ernie Els, Tiger Woods — and now Mike Weir.

The original minutes of the Royal Canadian Golf Association meeting of 1904 have disappeared and no one is sure what sparked the inauguration of the Open, but Karen Hewson, Director of the Canadian Golf Hall of Fame, speculates that there weren't enough professionals in Canada to make the championship viable until then. Grandly advertised as the Open Golf Championship of Canada, the first tournament was held at The Royal Montreal Golf Club on Saturday, July 2, a day after the Canadian Amateur championship was played.

The 1904 Open was a one-day, 36-hole, stroke-play tournament and the field included 10 pros and seven amateurs. The eventual winner was the unheralded John Oke, the club professional at (Royal) Ottawa, who had recently arrived from England. Playing in wet, miserable weather, Oke shot a 76 in the morning round to take a five-shot lead on the field. In the afternoon, he followed with an 80 for a two-stroke win over Percy Barrett, another English-born professional. Finishing in third place was legendary amateur George Lyon. The Open's total prize package was $170, which was divided among the top six professionals, with Oke earning $60 along with a gold medal. The top amateurs were rewarded with silverware.

The press was underwhelmed by Oke's victory. The *Globe* (forerunner to the *Globe and Mail*) buried the news between the junior lacrosse results and an advertisement for men's suspenders. The *Toronto Star*, which decided to run photographs of lawn bowlers on the opening page of its sports section, slid the results of the Open in next to a cure for ruptures. Still, the seeds had been sown and a century of the Open had begun.

CANADIAN CONTENT

The first decade of Opens was dominated by Canadian-based players. George Cumming arrived from Scotland in 1900, captured the 1905 Open and went on to become one of the most influential golfers in the country. As head professional at the Toronto Golf Club for nearly 50 years, Cumming turned out a succession of assistants who spread the golfing gospel across Canada. Charles and Albert Murray were British-born brothers who trained under Cumming and won four Open titles, alternating in 1906, 1908, 1911 and 1913 with two each. Karl Keffer was another Cumming protégé who captured the Open, in 1909 and 1914, and is the only Canadian-born winner to date. (Keffer was from Tottenham, Ontario.)

THE MYSTERIOUS J. DOUGLAS EDGAR

After an interruption of four years during WWI, the Open returned in 1919 with a strong international field. Played over the terrific Harry

1904 — J. H. OKE

Open Memories

A CENTURY *of* MEMORIES BEGAN *with the* FIRST CANADIAN OPEN

Played in drizzling rain over The Royal Montreal Golf Club's Dixie course, 17 players contested the first Open. The golfers played 36 holes in one day, the day after the Canadian Amateur championship. John H. Oke, originally from Britain and then serving as pro at the (Royal) Ottawa Golf Club, opened with a 76 and followed with an 80 in the afternoon to edge Lambton's Percy Barrett by two strokes. Oke's prize was $60 and a gold medal.

Open Memories

STRUCK BY RULE 19

At the 1983 Open, Andy Bean forgot his head, so to speak, and made an error that cost him a chance at the title. On the 15th hole, Bean tapped in a two-inch par putt with the handle of his putter. Unknowingly he had violated Rule 19, which states, "The ball shall be fairly struck at with the head of the club." Bean incurred a two-stroke penalty, which would haunt him in the final round the following day when he tied for fourth place with a course-tying 62, missing the John Cook-Johnny Miller playoff by two shots.

Colt-designed course at Hamilton, the favourite was "Long" Jim Barnes, a big-hitting Englishman then playing out of St. Louis, who would go on to win four majors in his career. The other player to make the headlines was Bobby Jones, who was dubbed "the boy wonder from Atlanta." The future icon of amateur golf and founder of the Masters was just 17 years old at the time and in the previous few years had been crisscrossing the eastern United States, playing in exhibition matches to raise funds for the Red Cross. It was to be Jones' only appearance at the Open.

The tournament's dark horse was another transplanted Englishman, J. Douglas Edgar. Originally from Newcastle, the 35-year-old Edgar, who had won the French Open in 1914 before disappearing into the trenches in the war, was now a club pro at Druid Hills Golf Club in Atlanta. A respected teacher, Edgar is credited with inventing the inside-out golf swing.

After the first two rounds, Edgar had built a nine-stroke advantage. Instead of sitting on his lead, however, Edgar pushed the edges of the golfing envelope, scorching the front nine with a 32 and adding a 34 on the back loop for a 66 and a total of 278, an astounding 16 strokes ahead of second-place finishers Jones and Keffer. The King Kong-sized winning margin is still a record for an Open championship.

In a radio interview he gave in 1943, Jones spoke about that extraordinary 1919 event and recalled that Edgar hadn't left his hotel room until the afternoon before the Open, and then only to hit three or four iron shots. Edgar explained to Jones that his hands felt thin, a mystical sensation that let him know that he was in possession of his A game and no further practice was needed.

Describing Edgar as "that strange and fascinating Englishman," Jones went on to say, "What a round that 66 was. I watched most of it and Douglas was simply playing tricks with the ball, bending it out of bounds to make it come in with a great run towards the green on a dogleg hole."

Edgar continued his Canadian domination the following year when he won the 1920 Open in a playoff at the Rivermead Golf Club in Ottawa. In July of 1921, the RCGA expected the defending champ to return to Canada and attempt to become the first player ever to take the Open title three times in a row. Edgar never showed up for the championship, and the RCGA later learned that he had decided to

Open Memories

TIGER WOODS' BUNKER SHOT *for* VICTORY *at the* 2000 BELL CANADIAN OPEN

Tiger Woods and Grant Waite staged a hole-by-hole battle over the final 18 holes of the 2000 Open at Glen Abbey Golf Club. When they arrived at the 18th, Woods found himself holding a slim one-stroke lead over the New Zealander. Tiger's drive found the right-side fairway bunker and it looked like the tournament was headed to a playoff. But Woods had other plans. With Waite on the green in two, Woods pulled out his 6-iron and took dead aim at the green. As his shot flew 216 yards to land just beyond the hole, the crowd went wild. He then chipped onto the green and sank his birdie putt to match Waite and win the title by a single stroke. With this victory and his U.S. and British Open wins, also in 2000, Tiger became the second person in golf history to win the Triple Crown.

1983 — JOHN COOK

Open Memories

JOHN COOK *and* JOHNNY MILLER REACH *a* SUDDEN DEATH FINISH—EVENTUALLY

Spectators at the 1983 Canadian Open thought the tournament would never end. PGA Tour star Johnny Miller and lesser-known John Cook both finished at 277 after four rounds at Glen Abbey Golf Club, while Jack Nicklaus just missed making it a three-way playoff by one stroke. But there was nothing "sudden" about the playoff that followed. Miller and Cook both recorded pars on the first playoff hole and moved on, matching each other's scores until finally, on the sixth, Cook sank his putt for a four—one better than Miller. The six-hole playoff remains the longest sudden-death playoff in Canadian Open history.

move his family back to Britain. He played in that summer's British Open at St. Andrews, then returned to Atlanta to finish out his contract at Druid Hills.

The news took a much more disturbing turn a few weeks later when the Atlanta police force reported that on the night of August 8, Douglas Edgar bled to death in front of his Atlanta home. The details were murky, but the local newspapers theorized that Edgar had either been hit by a drunk driver who failed to stop after the accident or he'd been the victim of a vicious mugging. Druid Hills offered a $500 reward for anyone who would come forward with information that would lead to the arrest of Edgar's killer. No one ever did and the case remains unsolved to this day.

THE DIEG AND THE SILVER SCOT

Throughout the next decade, the Open was dominated by two men, Leo Diegel and Tommy Armour. They were an odd golfing duo. Armour was a fiery Scot, war hero, best-selling author and legendary imbiber whose name still fronts a line of well-known golf clubs. Diegel holds the record of four Canadian Open titles and his career included 31 Tour wins, two PGA championships, four Ryder Cup appearances and induction into the World Golf Hall of Fame in 2003. Yet today, if Diegel is remembered at all, it is for his chicken wing putting style, twitchy tournament temperament and occasional last-minute collapse. He deserves better.

For reasons that Detroit native Diegel never figured out, the internal butterflies were never as thick in Canada. In 1924, the championship was held at the Mount Bruno Golf Club in Montreal. The 25-year-old Dieg was coming into the tournament on a high. The week before, he had captured the Shawnee Open in a playoff and was quickly gaining confidence in his unorthodox putting style. While critics made fun of his ungainly, elbows-out, standing-sitting stroke, Diegel was convinced that it was the definitive cure for the yips. "If it didn't look so terrible, all the boys would use it," he claimed.

Despite the non-believers, Diegel won his first Canadian Open with a two-stroke victory over Gene Sarazen. Diegel's idiosyncratic style endeared him to the gallery and 1,000 golf fans encircled the 18th green as he finished his final round. *Canadian Golfer* magazine reported, "When Diegel made the putt which earned him the championship, right lustily they cheered him. A gallery does love a game and cheerful fighter, and Diegel all through the tournament demonstrated that he was all that. His victory was a particularly popular one."

The Dieg repeated his championship the following year, when the Open was hosted at the Lambton Golf and Country Club in Toronto. Battling wet conditions and close friend Walter Hagen, Diegel hung on to take the title by a couple of strokes.

In 1928, the tournament was held at the Rosedale Golf Club, a Donald Ross-designed layout in north Toronto. Going into the final round, Hagen led the field—and Diegel—by three strokes, but this time it was Hagen who faltered, shooting a 73 while Diegel posted a four-under 68 to win the Open by two.

The following season, Diegel turned in one of the finest performances of his career at the Kanawaki Golf Club in Montreal. Shooting rounds of 70–67–71–66, he held off a charge by Tommy Armour and won his fourth Open title in five years with a record-breaking score of 274. To recognize his achievement, the RCGA presented Diegel with a replica of the championship's Rivermead Cup.

Tommy Armour's record in the Open is nearly as impressive as Diegel's, with three wins and two runner-up finishes. Born in Edinburgh in 1895, Armour served in the newly-formed British Tanks Corps during WWI, where he was decorated for heroism, earned a battlefield commission and rose to the rank of Major. Part of the Armour legend has it that the wee Scot once strangled an enemy commander with his bare hands, though his war came to an abrupt end during the Battle of Ypres in Belgium when his tank was slammed by heavy shelling and sprayed with a dose of deadly mustard gas. Armour was temporarily blinded by the gas and his shoulder was peppered with shrapnel. As part of his recovery therapy, Armour threw himself into golf, and by 1920, he was good enough to win the French Amateur title. That same year, he sailed across to Canada to begin his dazzling Open career.

Still playing as an amateur, Armour lost to Edgar in a playoff in the 1920 Open, then captured the title with victories in 1927 and 1930. In 1934, Armour was 39 years old and truly the Silver Scot. By taking advantage of the par fives at the Lakeview Golf Club, in the west end of Toronto, he won his third Open. After a career that included 22 tournament wins, including major wins at the British and U.S. and

1971 — LEE TREVINO

Open Memories

LEE TREVINO LEAVES LAUGHING

The 1971 Open at Richelieu Valley Golf Club in Montreal didn't win any points for style. Still, the course, the weather and a few other factors combined to make for a memorable tournament. On the last day, Lee Trevino "the Merry Mex" and former Canadian Open champion Art Wall Jr. went head-to-head in a playoff after finishing deadlocked at 275. In the playoff, a crowd swarmed the green before what could have been Wall's final putt. Wall missed the putt, and lost the championship to Trevino, who had captured the U.S. Open the week before and shortly after would win the British Open, becoming the first golfer to win all three national Open titles in a single year and give birth to the term "Triple Crown."

1985 — JACK NICKLAUS

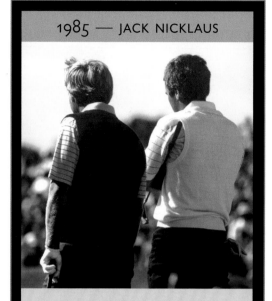

Open Memories

THE GOLDEN BEAR *and* MR. STRANGE

There is one record Jack Nicklaus probably wishes he didn't hold. Seven times he has been runner-up in the Canadian Open. None of them was perhaps as painful as the last, 20 years after the first. During the final round in 1985, Nicklaus teed off at the par-five 16th within one stroke of the leader, Curtis Strange. Looking at a 30-foot putt for an eagle, you could hear the proverbial pin drop as the gallery held its breath, all pulling for the 45-year-old Nicklaus. The putt, firmly struck, made its way toward the hole, but unfortunately it slid 18 inches past. Even more disappointing, Nicklaus' birdie putt missed and took along with it his chance to catch the leader.

PGA tourneys, Armour retired from competitive golf in 1936 to concentrate on a lucrative teaching career and to burnish his already growing legend. In *Golf's Greatest*, author Ross Goodner wrote of Armour, "Nothing was ever small about Tommy Armour's reputation. At one time or another he was known as the greatest iron player, the greatest raconteur, the greatest drinker and the greatest and most expensive teacher in golf."

HALL OF FAME DECADE

Despite the fact that North America was deeply mired in the Great Depression, the 1930s was one of the great periods for Open golf. Hall of Famers Tommy Armour, Walter Hagen, Lawson Little and Sam Snead all captured Canadian Open titles during the decade.

It was also when the tournament was bolstered by a sponsor. In the 1920s, the RCGA first began charging a $1 admission fee for the tournament. In the end though, ticket sales weren't enough to raise the kind of prize money that would attract the world's top-ranked players and leave money to fund the Association's commitments to amateur golf. In 1936, the Seagram Company became the Open's sponsor and provided the Seagram Gold Cup for the tournament's winner. In 1971, du Maurier took over the role of backer and introduced the tradition of presenting each winner with a piece of Inuit art. In 1994, Bell Canada answered the call and has been the tournament's title sponsor for the past decade, underwriting the millions of dollars now needed to host a PGA Tour event, as well as wiring up the Open with the latest in technology.

SLAMMIN' SAMMY COMES NORTH

In 1936, when Sam Snead teed it up at his first professional tournament, he sprayed his first two drives out of bounds. The pros who made up his foursome shook their heads and wondered what this hillbilly from Virginia was doing on the Tour. After all, it wasn't that many years before that Snead had been making his own clubs out of the swamp maples on his parents' farm. On his third attempt, though, Sam cranked his drive 350 yards, straight into the heart of the fairway. The Slammin' Sammy legend was born.

Possessor of the sweetest swing in golf, by 1938 the 26-year-old Snead was the Tour's leading money winner, finishing the year with

Open Memories

BYRON NELSON MAKES HISTORY

The 1945 Canadian Open knew it was facing a special challenge. Texan Byron Nelson was tearing up the PGA Tour. He had 10 consecutive victories under his belt by the time he arrived at the Thornhill Country Club in August. The course had been lengthened by 500 yards and par had been shaved to 70, but would the Stanley Thompson design be able to withstand the onslaught?

As it turned out, few managed to challenge par. Only Nelson and Vic Ghezzi came in under par (68) after the first round. Nelson managed his score in part due to an eagle on the 575-yard 14th. Ghezzi slipped in the second round, shooting a 77. During his second round, Nelson topped a drive and posted a double-bogey six on the second hole, and it looked like his streak might be over. But he fought back with three birdies on the back nine and finished at two over. Heading into Saturday's 36-hole final round, Nelson fired rounds of 72 and 68 to capture his 11th consecutive and, as it would turn out, final tournament of the 1945 season. During the nearly 50 years since, no golfer has come close to matching Nelson's record. Here, Nelson receives the trophy from E. Frowde Seagram.

Open Memories

WALTER HAGEN BARELY DEFEATS PERCY ALLIS

[or The Boston Tea Party Moves North]

Sheffield's Percy Allis (father of golf commentator Peter Allis) saved the reputation of British golf at the 1931 Canadian Open, even though he ultimately lost the championship. The British Ryder Cup team visited the Mississaugua Golf and Country Club to try for the title and achieved nothing of note. It was Allis, not a member of the team, playing in driving rain during the last round of the tournament, who shot 32 over the final nine holes to tie America's legendary Walter Hagen. During the 36-hole playoff, Allis led by one stroke after 18 holes, but in the afternoon Hagen shot a remarkable 68 to Allis's 70, winning the tournament by a stroke.

eight victories, including the Canadian Open. At the Mississaugua Golf and Country Club, which was that year's host, Snead played hard down the stretch, lassoing "Lighthorse" Harry Cooper and eventually beating him in a 27-hole playoff. (Lighthorse was no slouch—his Open record included wins in 1932 and 1937 and two second-place finishes.)

Snead didn't make the trip to Canada in 1939, when the Open was won by Jug McSpaden at the Riverside Country Club in Saint John, New Brunswick. The Slammer did return in 1940, however, to beat the defending champ in a playoff at the Scarboro Golf and Country Club. In 1941, Snead stretched his honeymoon to include a trip to the Lambton Golf and Country Club, where he made his new bride happy by defeating Canadian club pro Bob Gray—Snead's third win in four years.

The 1942 Open was played, but in 1943 the RCGA suspended the championship for the remainder of World War II.

As much as Snead dominated the tournament during his prime, his greatest Open feat took place 30 years later. Coming into the 1969 Open at Quebec's Pinegrove Country Club, the 57-year-old Snead had racked up nearly 140 worldwide victories. Tee to green, Snead could still keep up with the youngsters, but around the green he suffered from a big-league case of the yips. He even tried putting croquet style as a cure, though the United States Golf Association banned Snead's innovation, deeming it unnatural and somehow detrimental to the game.

At the 1969 Open, Snead regained his touch. But before the celebrations began, fellow southerner Tommy Aaron strode into the scorer's tent and signed for a course record of 64 and a tie for the lead. Snead, who was still in the tent, turned to Aaron and growled, "Why'd you pick this day to set a record? What the heck do you think you're doing? Man I'm tired." The next morning, Aaron, resplendent in beige shirt, beige pants and Clark Kent glasses, teed off against the colourful Snead in an 18-hole playoff. Aaron's younger legs carried him to a two-stroke victory. Ten years later, the 67-year-old Snead became the oldest golfer ever to make the cut at a PGA event by shooting his age in the second round. In the final round, he bettered it with a 66.

LORD BYRON RULES

Everybody knows that records are made to be broken, but on the PGA Tour, even the greatest players agree that a couple of marks are destined to stand the test of time. In 1945, Byron Nelson strung together a dream season, winning a total of 18 PGA-sanctioned events, with an incredible run of 11 straight victories. His 11th came at the Canadian Open, held at the Thornhill Country Club, north of Toronto.

Looking back on that stretch of superhuman golf, Nelson claimed that he sometimes played in a trance and in fact later admitted, "My game had gotten so good, there were times when I actually would get bored playing." When Nelson reached Toronto, tournament organizers had decided the man dubbed "Lord" Byron for his exquisite swing would be stirred from his near slumber. Nelson would have to earn his Canadian crown. The tight course was stretched an extra 500 yards and par was dropped by a stroke to 70. After firing rounds of 68, 72 and 72, Nelson pulled away from the pack with a final-round 68 and a four-stroke victory over Herman Barron. Nelson later said, "I wanted to win every important tournament on the PGA Tour, and I considered the Canadian Open one of those. It was a feather in my cap."

Ironically, just as Nelson was dominating the game, he was also planning his retirement. The Texas native had his heart set on buying a cattle ranch in the Lone Star State. "I had a whole collection of goals, but the ranch was number one," said Nelson. "It kept me going. Each win meant another cow, another 10 acres, a bigger down payment." In 1946, Nelson earned another five titles and then quit his full-time career on the PGA Tour for life on the farm.

MUFFIN FACE SHOWS HIS STUFF

Before Gary Player, Ernie Els and Retief Goosen, there was Bobby Locke. Born in Johannesburg, Locke dominated the South African golf scene in the late 1930s and then spent the war years piloting bombers on dangerous missions over Europe. At the end of the conflict, he picked up the sticks again and decided to try out his game in America.

Locke quickly stood out. Dressed in neckties and knickers and wielding a rusty-headed putter that his father had given him when he was nine, Locke proved that he had the game to compete in North

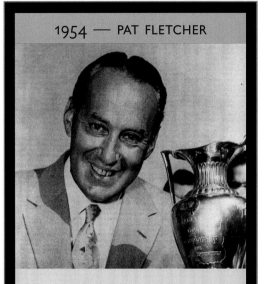

1954 — PAT FLETCHER

Open Memories

SASKATOON'S PAT FLETCHER CAPTURES THE CANADIAN OPEN

In 1914, Karl Keffer recorded his second Canadian Open victory. At the hosting Toronto Golf Club, he was cheered as the homegrown (and Torontonian) champion that he was. No one realized how long a drought it would be before the Open could lay claim to another Canadian champion. In 1954, when Pat Fletcher captured the Seagram Gold Cup at the Point Grey Golf and Country Club in Vancouver, the audience wasn't quite so naïve. There was jubilation that at long last, after 40 years, Canadians could salute one of her own. Fletcher's victory marked a brief respite in what would otherwise grow to a 90-year span of non-Canadian winners.

America. In a two-and-a-half-year stretch of playing on the PGA Tour, Locke, who was the greatest putter of his generation, amassed a record of 11 wins and 15 second-place finishes. One of his victories was the 1947 Canadian Open, played at the Scarboro Golf and Country Club, the A.W. Tillinghast-designed course in the east end of Toronto. Locke showed the classic course no mercy, posting four straight rounds in the 60s for a total of 268, a tournament scoring record.

Unfortunately, Locke's winning ways and idiosyncrasies didn't go over well with American pros, who nicknamed Locke "Muffin Face" for his unchangeable expression. The Tour suspended the South African in the fall of 1949 when he stayed in England to play some exhibition matches after winning his first British Open. Deciding to abandon his American career, Locke concentrated on the European Tour, where he won 23 times, collecting a total of four British Open titles and paving the way for the next wave of South African superstars.

ROCK 'N' ROLL GOLF

Social historians have mostly labelled the 1950s a bland, even repressed, decade. But for the Canadian Open, it was a time of youth and vitality. In 1956, Doug Sanders became the only amateur to win the Open. The 23-year-old, who would later distinguish himself with 20 Tour wins and a Day-Glo wardrobe, beat Dow Finsterwald in a playoff over the Beaconsfield Golf Club outside Montreal.

The very next season, teenager Bob Panasik not only entered the Open at the Westmount Golf and Country Club in Kitchener, but also he made the cut. The Windsor, Ontario native was only 15 years and eight months old at the time and still holds the record for the youngest player to ever make the cut at a PGA Tour event.

In 1954, Pat Fletcher thrilled the country when he became the first Canadian to win the Open in 40 years. At the Point Grey Golf and Country Club in Vancouver, Fletcher fired a spectacular 32 on the back nine of the final round, holding off fellow Canadian Gordie Brydson and Bill Welch to win the Open by four strokes. A club pro from the Saskatoon Golf and Country Club, Fletcher went on to become one of the country's most important professionals, serving as CPGA president from 1962 to 1965.

Open Memories

TOM WEISKOPF BEATS JACK NICKLAUS

Jack Nicklaus arrived at The Royal Montreal Golf Club for the 1975 Canadian Open as a favourite—as always. But this time he was truly at the top of his game. Winner of the Masters earlier in the year, he would go on to win three other tournaments and the PGA Championship that year, but not the Canadian Open. Coming to the final hole, Nicklaus thought he was leading Tom Weiskopf and Gay Brewer by a single shot. In reality, he had a more secure two-stroke advantage, but he felt he had to go for the green to guarantee a victory. Nicklaus hooked his drive into the water, and when Weiskopf birdied the 17th, a playoff was assured. On the first hole, Weiskopf made a birdie after Nicklaus missed a nine-footer and had to settle for his fourth of seven second-place finishes at the Open. Left to right: Jack Nicklaus, Pierre Dufault, Jack Heywood, Tom Weiskopf.

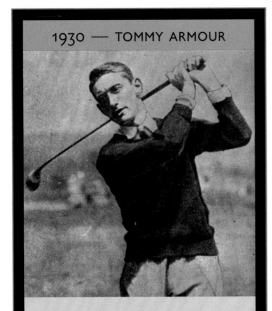

Open Memories

TOMMY ARMOUR PREVAILS *over* THE DIEG

At the 1930 Open, played at the Hamilton Golf and Country Club, four-time Canadian Open champion Leo Diegel was to face one-time Scottish war veteran and golfing legend Tommy Armour for the second time in as many years. In 1929, Diegel had prevailed, but 1930 would be a different story. The two arrived at the 72nd hole tied at 277, but Armour's route to his final score was the most remarkable. Shooting a total of 213 over the first three rounds, he swept his way to the tie with a stunning 64 for his final 18 holes — a record for the Hamilton club that stood until 1991. In the 36-hole playoff Armour proved his mettle by shooting 138 to Diegel's 141.

But the apex of the golfing decade took place in 1955. While Elvis was about to kick-start a new revolution in music, Arnold Palmer was about to do the same for the golfing world. The future King of Golf didn't wiggle his hips, but he did hitch up his pants, waggle his blacksmith-sized forearms and launch his version of rock 'n' roll golf. Even better, Arnie still hasn't left the building.

After stints at Wake Forest University and with the U.S. Coast Guard, Palmer emerged from Pennsylvania steel country and onto the national scene in 1954 with his unexpected win at the U.S. Amateur. Not long afterwards, he took major life steps by turning professional and eloping with Winnie Walzer.

In the days before Arnie could afford to zip through the skies in his private jet, he and Winnie crisscrossed the continent by car like a couple of golfing gypsies. In the weeks leading up to the Canadian Open, Palmer zigzagged from his hometown of Latrobe, Pennsylvania, to the U.S. Open in San Francisco, up the west coast to Portland and Vancouver, then back across to Minnesota, Milwaukee, Toledo, Chicago and finally the Weston Golf and Country Club in Toronto, where they camped out in the field behind the course superintendent's shed. While Palmer had made some money on his 3,000-mile loop of North America, he admitted that if he didn't earn some bigger cheques soon, he'd have to consider returning to Pennsylvania to find a job as a club pro.

The Weston course, which the year before had been whacked hard by Hurricane Hazel, was receptive to low scores. First-round leader Charlie Sifford fired a 63 — a new course record — but Palmer followed closely with a 64. Foreshadowing things to come, the PGA rookie then began a torrid run, adding a 67 and another 64 to lead the field by six.

Arnie was assigned a caddie by the name of Ray Slater, a Weston member who had volunteered to work the tournament for the week. According to the Weston club history, for the first two rounds, Arnie waved off any advice from Slater. At the seventh hole of the third round Palmer asked for some help. The caddie advised using the 4-wood to reach the par-five in two, and when Palmer launched the ball with his customary fervour, it sailed over the green, smacking a member of the gallery in the head. It was the last time that Slater was summoned for advice. (As usual with a Palmer story, it finishes with a happy ending: at the time, amateur golfers weren't allowed to accept money for caddying in professional events. Instead, the generous Palmer paid Slater's Weston golf fees for the following season.)

During the final round, Palmer cruised around the course, his only hiccup coming at Weston's fifth hole, a treacherous par-four that bends left off the tee, with a green notched into a hill overlooking a creek and gully. Arnie snap-hooked his drive into the trees. He found his ball but was undecided about what shot to play next. His impatient playing partner, "Terrible" Tommy Bolt, finally blurted out, "For God's sake, Arnie. Chip it out into the fairway. You've got a six-stroke lead." Knowing that accepting advice from anyone but your caddie is a two-stroke penalty, Palmer decided instead to punch the ball through a gap in the trees. Weston member and marshal Tom Warrington moved a dead tree in Palmer's way and Arnie made it through the gap. "My dad helping Arnie with the tree became an important part of our family history," says Warrington's son, Doug, who adds, "After Dad passed away, we planted a tree on the fifth hole to commemorate his life and small part in Arnie's victory."

Palmer steadied himself after the fifth hole and finished with a 70 and a total score of 265, still the second-lowest total ever recorded in the Open. Fittingly, the 1955 tournament was the first Open to be televised across the country. Canadians from coast to coast saw the baby-faced Palmer engulfing Winnie in a joyous hug. Neither had an inkling of how much their lives would soon change.

After the ceremony, Arnie and Winnie once again packed up the car and this time headed out to a fishing camp just east of Toronto where they intended to relax for a couple of days before heading to Montreal for the Labatt tournament. In his autobiography, Palmer reflected on that golden day. "I was the new Canadian Open champion, I'd won my first PGA Tour event and, sitting on the end of a small dock fishing and drinking cold beers in the beautiful summer dusk, I couldn't have felt happier or more at peace."

NICKLAUS NORTH

Jack Nicklaus holds hundreds of golfing records, but there's one that he'd gladly forfeit.

Jack started coming north in 1962, but instead of holding the record for the number of times he's won our Open, he owns the

Open Memories

GREG NORMAN REELS IT IN

The 1992 Canadian Open at Glen Abbey Golf Club was the scene of a recovery and history revisited. Greg Norman, better known as "The Shark," arrived deep into a two-year winless drought. On Sunday, Norman lost a three-shot lead on the back nine and watched two-time champion Bruce Lietzke sink his putt for a birdie on 18 to force a playoff. On the second playoff hole, Norman hit a 3-wood over the pond at 18 into the back bunker, splashed out to three feet and sank his birdie putt for the win. How important was this victory to Norman? In the press room, he claimed, "Right now, I'd say this one is bigger than the British Open... I needed it. I needed it bad."

title for being the king of second-place finishers. Seven times he's come away as a bridesmaid.

Looking back on those seven Opens, there is no pattern to Nicklaus' defeats. Sometimes he stumbled; other times destiny had already picked another winner. The Golden Bear has called the Open "The one significant championship I've never won."

Jack's first real run at the Canadian title was in 1965, at the Mississaugua Golf and Country Club. The first three days were dominated by Australian Bruce Devlin, who went into Saturday's final round at five-under-par with a two-stroke lead on Mason Rudolph, Gene Littler and favourites Palmer and Nicklaus. Then Devlin quickly bailed out of the lead by bogeying the first three holes. Palmer and Nicklaus were paired together and the gallery anticipated a head-to-head slugfest, but Arnie's putter wouldn't cooperate and he limped home with a 76. Instead, Nicklaus' competition came from Gene "The Machine" Littler.

Jack went into the back nine with a one-stroke lead but lost it—and probably the championship—at the 537-yard, par-five 12th hole. Known by Mississaugua members as "Big Chief," the hole's narrow green is guarded by a creek. Undaunted, the young Golden Bear called for his 3-wood, determined to carry the water, a daunting 240-yard carry into the wind. Nicklaus took his usual Herculean swipe, but it wasn't enough and his ball hit the bank and rolled back into the creek. Jack bogeyed the hole and Littler, who was in the following group, laid up, methodically stroked in his birdie and eventually beat Nicklaus by a single stroke.

"I thought of laying the ball up, but I didn't see the point in it," Nicklaus later told reporters. "I believe in playing bold and I would play that hole the same way again," said the runner-up without regret.

The 1975 Open at The Royal Montreal Golf Club is the one Jack admits he should have won. Standing on the 18th tee during the final round, the Golden Bear enjoyed a two-stroke lead over Tom Weiskopf and Gay Brewer. But this was in the days before instant communication. Jack thought he was only one up and felt he had to birdie 18 to ensure the victory. Instead of playing it safe, he hooked his drive into the water and Weiskopf birdied 17 to set up a playoff. The sudden death was staged over the 414-yard, par-four 15th hole. Both players hit good drives and Weiskopf lofted a perfect 7-iron

Open Memories

ARNOLD PALMER STARTS *on* HIS WAY

The 1955 Canadian Open, at the Weston Golf and Country Club, was the first time the tournament would be televised from coast to coast. It was a terrific opportunity to showcase the national Open to all areas of the country, but it was made that much better by a charismatic young player who came up from Pennsylvania and took the title. The young Arnold Palmer had only recently turned professional. He and his wife Winnie were coming to the end of their funds and he'd have to go home and take up a club pro position if he didn't soon start cashing cheques. As it happened, Palmer needn't have worried. He won the title by four strokes and recorded the first of his 62 PGA Tour victories.

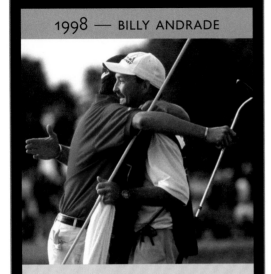

Open Memories

BILLY ANDRADE HOLDS TIGHT

It wasn't pretty, but then again all they remember is who won. In 1998, Billy Andrade and Bob Friend were both in contention all weekend at Glen Abbey Golf Club. With a one-shot advantage heading to the 72nd hole, Andrade went for the green in two and his approach from 237 yards found the pond in front of the green. His fourth shot landed 30 feet from the hole, but, amazingly, Andrade made the putt for par to force a playoff. The playoff wasn't a classic by any stretch of the imagination. The approach shots on 18 by both players ended up in the gallery, and when Friend's chip shot rolled off the green and into the water, Andrade played it safe and claimed the title.

that covered the flag for a tap-in birdie. Nicklaus missed a nine-footer and settled for par and his fourth runner-up finish.

Jack's last realistic shot at winning the title took place at Glen Abbey in 1985. He'd come to Toronto in the middle of a golfing funk. In June, he'd missed the cut at the U.S. Open and decided to take a break from the game and fly up to New Brunswick for some salmon fishing. The therapy worked. In the third round, the 45-year-old shot a 66, putting him in third spot, a stroke behind Greg Norman and two behind leader Curtis Strange.

The new Big Three made up the final group, and while the younger guys turned some heads, the heart of the gallery was solidly behind Nicklaus. "They were rooting so damn hard for the poor guy," remembered Strange. Thousands of them held their breath on the par-five 16th hole when their idol stood over a 30-foot eagle putt. If he sank it, he'd take the lead from Strange. Nicklaus struck the ball boldly and slid it just 18 inches past the cup. Then, to the disbelief of the gallery, he missed the tap-in birdie putt. The gallery wilted, as did Jack's chances. He bogeyed 17 and parred 18 to end up tied with Norman, two back of Strange, who would win the Open again in 1987.

Realizing that this might be one of his last chances of winning the Open, a downcast Nicklaus commented, "I had every opportunity to win the golf tournament. Obviously, I'm very, very disappointed." But the long list of Open disappointments hadn't dampened his enthusiasm for the tournament. "I'd love to win the Canadian Open. That's one of the reasons I keep coming back. You keep coming back until you win it," said Nicklaus, adding, "I hope I'm not playing in the Canadian Open when I'm 80."

THE GLEN ABBEY STORY

While it's unlikely that Nicklaus will still be pursuing the Open as an octogenarian, the Golden Bear has already put his indelible paw print on the tournament. In June of 1976, the RCGA and Nicklaus unveiled Glen Abbey Golf Club, which was to become the Open's primary home for the next quarter of a century. It was Nicklaus' first solo design project, and it was a tricky assignment. The public course needed to be tough enough to challenge the game's biggest hitters and at the same time give the average golfer some fun. And for the first time anywhere, the course had to incorporate stadium-style architecture so Open fans could be guaranteed up-close-and-personal views at tournament time.

Glen Abbey has been a success on those levels, especially during tournament week, when thousands of fans have jammed the hillside at 18 to watch some of the game's most dramatic finishes.

LEE WEARS THE TRIPLE CROWN

Lee Trevino is one of the great stories in all of sports. Surviving a hardscrabble upbringing that even Charles Dickens would have had trouble describing, struck by lightning at the height of his career, then losing a couple of personal fortunes, Trevino persevered and is always the gallery's favourite, especially in Canada.

The Canadian Open played a major part in Lee Trevino's amazing four-week stretch of golf during the summer of 1971. On June 21, Trevino beat Nicklaus in an 18-hole playoff at Merion to win the U.S. Open. Two weeks later, a tired Super Mex arrived at Montreal's Richelieu Valley Golf Club with time for only one practice round, though, as usual, he made room for quotables. "These French girls in their hot pants are driving me crazy," admitted Lee, who then looked across at wife Claudia and added, "I've got to win this tournament. Claudia's already spent the money."

And that's just what he did. After a poor first round of 73, Trevino shot a 68 on Friday and added course-record-tying 67s on the final two rounds. It was enough to catch 1960 champion Art Wall Jr., whom Trevino beat in the first hole of the playoff. Dashing out of the clubhouse to catch a plane for England, he stopped long enough to scribble a note, saying, "I used this locker and won—Lee Trevino." Within 24 hours, Trevino was playing a practice round at Royal Birkdale, wearing an Expos ball cap. By the end of the week, he had captured the British championship, becoming the first golfer ever to win the U.S., Canadian and British Opens in the same season. Looking back on his Triple Crown year, Trevino said, "The Canadian Open is one of the world's oldest championships and I rate it among the top four in the world." Du Maurier later presented Trevino with a massive trophy to mark the Triple Crown win.

Trevino went on to win the inaugural Open at Glen Abbey in 1977, when the course set up nicely for his patented fade. Two years

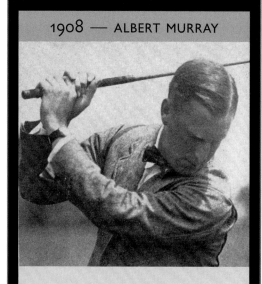

1908 — ALBERT MURRAY

Open Memories

THE YOUNGEST CHAMPION

The Murrays moved to Canada when youngest son Albert was a baby. Raised in Toronto, across from the original site of the Toronto Golf Club, he and older brother Charles saw an opportunity to make some money and have some fun being caddies. Charles went to the club first and became an assistant to pro George Cumming. Albert took after his brother, first at Toronto and then Montreal. When the first Canadian Open was played at The Royal Montreal Golf Club, Albert again followed his brother and played in the championship—at the age of 16. When the tournament returned to Royal Montreal in 1908, Murray became, at 20, the youngest player ever to win the Canadian Open.

later, Lee picked up his third Open title, using a putter he bought from a fan in the Glen Abbey gallery for $75. Going into the final round, it looked like the Open belonged to Tom Watson, the Tour's dominant player in the late 1970s. Teeing off with a three-stroke lead, Watson steered his tee shot into the bulrushes at the par-three third hole. Unbelievably, he made the identical swing on his next attempt. This time, Tom Terrific was able to splash the ball onto the green, finishing with a triple-bogey six. Watson whimpered home with a 78 to finish third, the closest he would ever come to winning the Canadian Open.

NORMAN CONQUEST

All golfers will acknowledge that you need a break or two to win a title. For Greg Norman, the rabbit's foot didn't appear at the 1984 Open until the second-last hole of the tournament. After putting together a string of wins on the Asia/Australian and European Tours in the early 1980s, The Shark was playing his first full year in America. Coming into Canada, he'd crushed the field at the Kemper Open with a five-stroke victory and lost a playoff to Fuzzy Zoeller in the U.S. Open.

Norman kept the momentum flowing across the 49th parallel. During the final round, at Glen Abbey's 17th hole, a pumped-up Shark smacked his approach shot over the green and into a temporary parking lot that hadn't been marked as out of bounds but normally would have been. Fortunately Norman could therefore play his ball without penalty. Even better, a marshall in the gallery owned the car under which The Shark's ball was lodged. She moved the car and he pitched onto the green and two-putted for a bogey. Norman finished with a 67 and a two-stroke win over Nicklaus. For Canadians, the bright light was Vancouver's Richard Zokol, who finished in fifth place, one of the best Canuck showings since Pat Fletcher's win in 1954.

Times had changed when Norman returned for the Open at Glen Abbey in 1992. The Shark was suffering from his first golfing drought—he'd been winless for more than two years. Tips on putting from a Toronto friend got Norman back in the swim and he beat two-time Canadian Open champ Bruce Lietzke in a playoff. "It was like somebody put a coin in the jukebox and the right song started playing," said Norman after the win. The next year, Norman won both Doral and the British Open.

Open Memories

ISLAND HOPPING WITH PAT FITZSIMMONS

At the 1975 Open at The Royal Montreal Golf Club, Pat Fitzsimmons' shot on the 16th hole found an unusual landing spot—a small island in the water hazard. Reluctant to forfeit his ball and incur a penalty stroke, Fitzsimmons convinced his caddy to carry him to the island. He went on to par the hole.

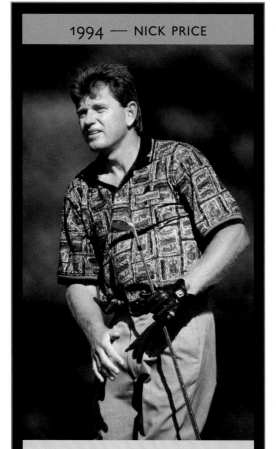

1994 — NICK PRICE

Open Memories

NICK PRICE DOUBLES THE PLEASURE

When Nick Price won the 1991 Canadian Open, he did it by tearing up the valley holes of Glen Abbey. In 1994, his victory hinged on an amazingly accurate and long 2-iron on the par-five 16th hole. On the first hole after leaving the valley, Price's shot finished just two feet from the hole. He sank the putt for an eagle and won the championship, handing Mark Calcavecchia his second runner-up finish in five years.

THE PRICE IS RIGHT

Nick Price shatters the adage that nice guys finish last. Throughout the 1990s, the perennial good guy was the most successful player on the planet, with 16 victories on the PGA Tour, three wins in the majors and two Canadian Open titles.

Price admits to having a soft spot for our Open. "The Canadian Open has always been very special to me. It was the first tournament I played on the PGA Tour back in 1984." And he nearly won that 1984 tournament but stumbled down the stretch.

In 1991, Price made sure there was no repeat collapse and instead fired a flashy final-round 66, which included birdies on all five of Glen Abbey's valley holes, for a one-stroke victory over David Edwards.

In 1994, Price was enjoying a career year with summertime wins at both the British Open and PGA Championship. By September, though, he was so burnt out that he contemplated heading home and skipping Canada altogether. Fortunately, Price's usual nice guy persona kicked in and he made the trip to Glen Abbey, where his final two rounds of 68 carried him to a one-stroke win over Mark Calcavecchia. The highlight was Price's laser 2-iron on the 16th hole, a 516-yard par-five. The ball stopped two feet from the hole and the tap-in eagle sealed the win.

REDEMPTION SONG

Norman isn't the only veteran who has used the Open to relaunch his career. Throughout the 1990s, players like David Frost, Mark O'Meara, Steve Jones, Billy Andrade and Hal Sutton all captured Open titles. For O'Meara, his win in 1995 sparked a career comeback that led to wins at both the Masters and British Open in 1998. Sutton's payoff was immediate. Two weeks after winning at Glen Abbey, Sutton went 3–1–1 in his Ryder Cup matches, leading the American team to a victory over the Europeans at Brookline. Sutton later said, "That [Canadian Open victory] had a great deal to do with what I did at the Ryder Cup. The American players hadn't won many tournaments going into the Ryder Cup. It fell at the right time. To leave tournament golf with that in your head going into the Ryder Cup was really big."

The 1996 Open will always be remembered as the year two supernatural forces blew into Glen Abbey. As Hurricane Fran was working her way up the eastern seaboard, Tiger Woods touched down in Toronto, making golf fans of all ages weak in the knees. Playing in only his second tournament as a pro, the 20-year-old, who had become an icon as an amateur, was determined to show that he belonged with the big boys.

Woods shot a roller-coaster round of four birdies, an eagle, two bogeys, a double bogey and a handful of 350-yard drives for a two-under-par 70. "With all that trouble, I was pretty happy with my round. I didn't blow myself out of the tournament. It was an adventure," said Woods, who went on to say, "The crowds were really neat and they actually helped me find my ball a few times."

By Saturday morning, the weather had taken over the front pages. Fran ripped and roared through Toronto, knocking down trees and power lines and submerging Glen Abbey's greens. For the only time in its 72-hole history, the Open was shortened to only three rounds.

On Sunday, Tiger fired a 68, the best score of the day, and finished in 11th place behind winner Dudley Hart, whose 68–64–70–202 was good enough to win by a stroke over David Duval.

The very next year, the Bell Canadian Open became the only professional tournament where Tiger Woods missed a cut. At the 1997 Open, hosted at The Royal Montreal Golf Club, Woods had trouble with the heavy, rough and narrow fairways, shooting 70–76 to miss the weekend by a stroke.

By 2000, Tiger had tweaked the last few imperfections in his game and was playing in the golfing version of a state of grace. By the end of the season, he had set or tied 27 PGA Tour records, won nine tournaments, captured three straight majors (the U.S. Open, the British Open and the PGA Championship) and earned over US$9 million in a single season. His last tournament victory of the season, the Bell Canadian Open, punctuated his historic year. Unlike most of his wins in 2000, where he carried a comfortable lead into the final round, Woods was forced to go hammer and tongs with New Zealander Grant Waite all day long. On the 18th hole, it looked like Tiger had finally blinked when he dumped his drive into the right-side bunker. With 50,000 people looking on, Woods calmly dug into

2000 — COREY PAVIN

Open Memories

COREY PAVIN TIES RECORD

At the 2000 Bell Canadian Open, Corey Pavin became just the sixth golfer in PGA Tour history to take only 18 putts over one round. Pavin tied the mark during the second round as he shot a 65. Unfortunately, he was unable to keep his hot putter going and ended up finishing tied for 42nd. Since then, no one else has been able to join the group that includes Pavin, Sam Trahan, Mike McGee, Kenny Knox, Andy North and Jim McGovern.

the bunker and then blasted a 6-iron 216 yards over the water to within 18 feet of the hole. "When pressure is at its peak, that's when your concentration is at its highest," said Woods of his miracle shot. After a chip and a putt for a birdie, Tiger had posted a 65 to Waite's 66, winning the tournament and the Triple Crown by a single stroke.

21ST CENTURY

As the Open moved into the 21st century, it continued to produce amazing stories. In 2002, when the tournament was played for the first time at Angus Glen Golf Club in Markham, Ontario, journeyman Neal Lancaster looked like he had a lock on hoisting the trophy. After all, going into the final hole the North Carolina native with a voice as thick as molasses led the field by two strokes. But Lancaster felt the heat, double-bogeyed the 18th and lost the Open in a playoff to John Rollins. The good-natured Lancaster later reflected on his defeat by saying, "The way I look at it is, the only reason it happened to me is 'cause the good Lord knew I could handle it." In 2003, the Open was again forced to a playoff where veteran Bob Tway scooped up the US$756,000 first-prize cheque by edging all-world putter Brad Faxon.

The 2003 Open was an unqualified success. The host course, the Hamilton Golf and Country Club, was given rave reviews by players and fans, tickets were sold out, television ratings soared 215% and the gallery supported homegrown Canadians as never before. Mike Weir, who finished 10th, said of his Hamilton experiences, "Speaking of the fans, they were wonderful all week. I don't think I've ever had so many standing ovations as I got this week. They'd cheer me when I walked to the range, when I warmed up, on every tee and green — they even cheered me when I came out of the Port-O-Let."

Just as telling was the comment by Charles Howell III, one of the game's most promising young guns: "I would give my left arm to win this tournament. It's the Canadian Open; it is the country's national open."

With that kind of enthusiasm from the fans and the game's new stars, the Bell Canadian Open is in good shape as it heads into its next 100 years.

Open Memories

AUSSIE TAKES TITLE, *while the* GOLDEN BEAR MISSES OUT AGAIN

The 1984 Canadian Open was truly an international affair. Australian Greg Norman took the title with a 278 over Glen Abbey Golf Club, keeping the title from Jack Nicklaus yet again. But another, then little-known, character was also in contention—27-year-old Zimbabwe native Nick Price held the lead for two rounds with back-to-back 67s. In the third round, Price slipped with a 73 but managed to hold on to his lead. His playing partners over the final two rounds, Nicklaus and Norman, garnered a lot of attention, and this may have ended the young golfer's hopes of a victory as he shot a final-round 76 to end five strokes behind Norman. Yet another young man also announced his presence that year, former Canadian Amateur champion Richard Zokol. With a tie for fifth place, Zokol finished as the top Canadian.

THE HOST CLUBS

The Royal Montreal Golf Club

by RANDY PHILLIPS

Established in 1873, and awarded the "Royal" part of its name in 1884 by Queen Victoria, The Royal Montreal Golf Club was the first permanent golf club in the western hemisphere. Long considered one of the top courses in Canada, it has, perhaps surprisingly, played host to the Canadian Open only nine times in the 100-year history of the championship. Nevertheless, Royal Montreal, where Englishman John H. Oke won the first Canadian Open, a 36-hole stroke-play championship held on July 2, 1904, has witnessed some of the most memorable moments in the country's national Open.

The foremost of these came to pass in the 1975 championship, where golf legend Jack Nicklaus came closest to winning the one title that would elude his grasp during a three-decade career on the PGA Tour, though he finished second in the Canadian Open a record seven times.

Playing the Blue Course, the more renowned of two championship courses at Royal Montreal, Nicklaus lost to Tom Weiskopf

ABOVE In the 1890s, The Royal Montreal Golf Club's Dixie course was conveniently located near the railroad station to allow easy access in the days before the automobile was a common possession. But by 1950 this proximity had its own drawbacks. As that year's Canadian Open drew near, members of the club were increasingly concerned that trains would distract the players, especially on the fourth hole, shown here. There was great relief—and some irony— when Canada's railways suffered their first major labour dispute at the same time as the Open was played, silencing the rails.

OPPOSITE 16th hole at The Royal Montreal Golf Club, the Blue Course, Île Bizard.

ABOVE The field for the 1913 Canadian Professional Golfers' Association Championship, pictured at Beaconsfield Golf Club, closely resembles the one that challenged for the Canadian Open, just up the road at the Royal Montreal the same year.

on the first hole of a sudden-death playoff. Nicklaus and Weiskopf had both shot course-record five-under-par 65s in the first round of the 72-hole championship and Nicklaus started the final round at seven-under, one shot ahead of Weiskopf. At the 18th hole, Nicklaus thought he still had a single-stroke lead. In fact, he was two strokes ahead, but he decided to use his driver to secure his position, a par-four dogleg. He drove his tee shot into the water on the left side of the fairway and finished with a bogey. Weiskopf birdied 17.

The playoff started and ended on the par-four 15th, the most spectacular hole on the course. Nicklaus missed a nine-foot putt for birdie, while Weiskopf made his from three feet to win the Canadian Open for the second time in three years. Years later, Nicklaus said: "Had I known I was two strokes ahead, I would have used a 3-wood."

In addition to 1904 and 1975, Royal Montreal played host to Canadian Opens in 1908, 1913, 1926, 1950, 1975, 1980, 1997 and 2001, though urban development forced the club to relocate twice, first from its original location at the foot of Mount Royal in the heart of the city, then from the West Island area in Dorval known as Dixie. In

1959, it finally settled in to its current location on Île Bizard, a few miles west of downtown Montreal, and in 1980 became the last alternative venue before the championship took up what was then thought to be permanent residence at Glen Abbey. And in 1997, when the RCGA decided to once again begin staging the national Open at different courses in Ontario and Quebec and eventually across the country, Royal Montreal was again the first choice.

The 1997 Open at Royal Montreal will long be remembered not for who won (Steve Jones) or who didn't win, but for who didn't make the cut—Tiger Woods. After an opening round of par 70 on the 6,810-yard Blue Course, the reigning Masters champion shot 76 in the second round for a 146 total and missed the 36-hole cut by two shots—the first cut Woods had missed since he turned pro in late August of the previous year. After that, the world's number-one-ranked player would put together an impressive string of consecutive cuts made that saw him break the legendary Byron Nelson's all-time record of 113 by the end of the 2003 season.

ABOVE The founding of The Royal Montreal Golf Club was imaginatively portrayed in this composite image of the founding members and others on the original playing field on Mount Royal.

THE ROYAL MONTREAL GOLF CLUB

Dixie, South Course   YARDAGE: 5,665   PAR: N/A   DESIGNER: Willie Dunn

1904   FORMAT: 36 holes, 1 day   PURSE: $170, 1st place $60
       DATE: July 2   WINNER: J.H. Oke, *(Royal) Ottawa Golf Club*   156
       FIELD: 17   RUNNER-UP: Percy Barrett, *Lambton Golf & Country Club*   158

1908   FORMAT: 72 holes, 2 days   PURSE: $225, 1st place N/A
       DATE: June 28–29   WINNER: Albert Murray, *Outremont Golf Club*   300
       FIELD: 30   RUNNER-UP: George Sargent, *(Royal) Ottawa Golf Club*   304

1913   FORMAT: 72 holes, 2 days   PURSE: N/A
       DATE: August 14–15   WINNER: Albert Murray, *Kanawaki Golf Club*   295
       FIELD: 30   RUNNER-UP: Nicol Thompson, *Hamilton Golf & Country Club* 301

Dixie, Revamped South Course   YARDAGE: 6,522   PAR: 72

1926   FORMAT: 72 holes (18, 18, 36), 3 days   PURSE: $1,575, 1st place N/A
       DATE: August 5–7   WINNER: MacDonald Smith, *Lakeville, NY*   283
       FIELD: 54   RUNNER-UP: Gene Sarazen, *Fresh Meadows, Long Island*   286

1950   FORMAT: 72 holes, 4 days   PURSE: $10,000, 1st place $2,000
       DATE: August 24–27   WINNER: Jim Ferrier, *San Francisco, California*   271
       FIELD: 200   RUNNER-UP: Ted Kroll, *New Hartford, New York*   274

Blue Course, Île Bizard   DESIGNER: Dick Wilson

1975   FORMAT: 72 holes, 4 days   PURSE: $200,000, 1st place $40,000
       DATE: July 24–27   WINNER: Tom Weiskopf, *Columbus, Ohio*   274
       YARDAGE: 6,628   PAR: 70   RUNNER-UP: Jack Nicklaus, *Muirfield Village, Ohio*   274
       FIELD: 153   CUT: 71 players at 144   Weiskopf won sudden-death playoff with a birdie

1980   FORMAT: 72 holes, 4 days   PURSE: $350,000, 1st place $63,000
       DATE: June 19–22   WINNER: Bob Gilder, *Cornwallis, Oregon*   274
       YARDAGE: 6,628   PAR: 70   RUNNERS-UP: Leonard Thompson, *Orlando, Florida*   276
       FIELD: 156   CUT: 73 players at 147   Jerry Pate, *Pensacola, Florida*   276

1997   FORMAT: 72 holes, 4 days   PURSE: $1,500,000, 1st place $270,000
       DATE: September 1–7   WINNER: Steve Jones, *Phoenix, Arizona*   275
       YARDAGE: 6,810   PAR: 70   RUNNER-UP: Greg Norman, *Hobe Sound, Florida*   276
       FIELD: 156   CUT: 74 players at 144

2001   FORMAT: 72 holes, 4 days   PURSE: $3.8 million, 1st place $684,000
       DATE: September 3–9   WINNER: Scott Verplank, *Edmond, Oklahoma*   266
       YARDAGE: 6,859   PAR: 70   RUNNERS-UP: Joey Sindelar, *Horseheads, New York*   269
       FIELD: 156   CUT: 77 players at 141   Bob Estes, *Austin, Texas*   269

NOTE: Where Par is marked with N/A it was not a common practice to assign "par"
for the course until following the War.

PREVIOUS PAGE The last Open played at the Royal Montreal's Dixie course brought crowds unlike anything seen in the earliest years of the championship. Here the clubhouse provides a backdrop for the 18th hole and the many keen fans of the game who would watch Jim Ferrier win the first of his back-to-back titles.

ABOVE Tom Weiskopf spent most of his career in the shadow of fellow Ohio State alum Jack Nicklaus, but not at the Canadian Open. Weiskopf won a pair of Open titles, including 1975 at Royal Montreal. A 16-time winner on the PGA Tour, he won only one major (the 1973 British Open), but was a four-time runner-up at the Masters.

RIGHT The Open had been moved to its semi-permanent home at Glen Abbey in 1977, so the return to the Royal Montreal in 1980 was a special event. The Île Bizard location welcomed the players back and 29-year-old Bob Gilder won the title, one of six he would claim on the PGA Tour.

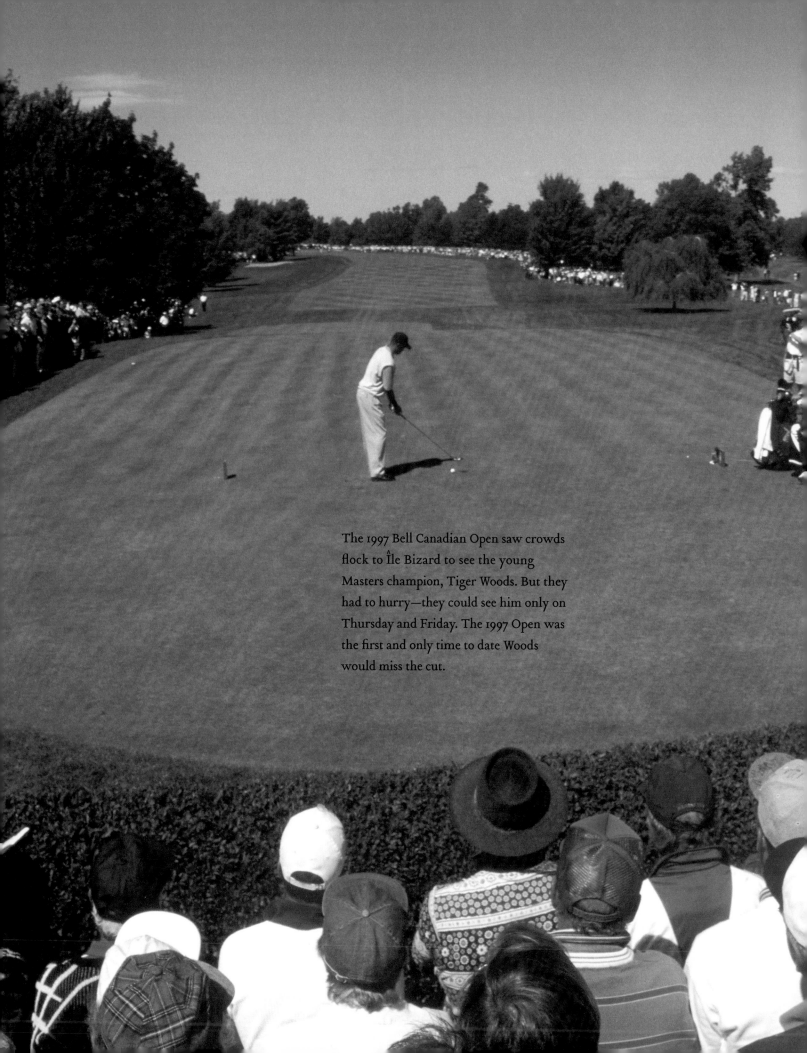

The 1997 Bell Canadian Open saw crowds flock to Île Bizard to see the young Masters champion, Tiger Woods. But they had to hurry—they could see him only on Thursday and Friday. The 1997 Open was the first and only time to date Woods would miss the cut.

The 1989 Canadian Open champion, Steve Jones, matched Greg Norman's record as the player with the longest gap between Canadian titles. In 1997, Jones came to the front and, as fate would have it, defeated Norman by a single stroke for the title.

Newsmaker John Daly came to Île Bizard in 2001 and was a crowd favourite at the Bell Canadian Open. He didn't win, but he did showcase his new and improved game, finishing just back of the leaders.

Each year, Canadians watch the beginning of the Open with a hope that maybe this year the champion will break the long stretch since the last Canadian victor. In 2001, fans were served up a surprise when Ontario's David Morland IV was in contention on Sunday. As those hopes slipped away over the last few holes, they weren't dashed but postponed . . . to the next year.

A 37-year-old Texan defeated a Tiger— and the rest of the field—to capture the 2001 title and validate his selection as the captain's pick on that year's Ryder Cup team. Scott Verplank's sense of humour was in full play when he posed for this shot with some RCMP officers.

Toronto Golf Club

by KAREN HEWSON

The Toronto Golf Club hosted the Canadian Open five times, twice on its original course on Kingston Road and thrice at the present location, the H. S. Colt-designed course on Dixie Road. Home professional George Cumming won the first Open played over the club, but his student Karl Keffer won it the next two times—once on the Kingston Road and once on the Dixie Road location—leaving his teacher in the runner-up position. W. H. Trovinger captured the Open in 1921 and in 1927, the Toronto club again hosted the tournament. This time Tommy Armour, runner-up in the 1920 championship, took the title.

Here's how the 1905 tournament was reported in a Toronto newspaper:

> The open championship and annual handicap competitions were decided as the closing events of the Golf Tournament, concluded last Saturday on the Toronto Club links.

ABOVE George Cumming came to Canada from Dumfries, Scotland. Hired by the Toronto Golf Club to serve as its professional in 1900, and winner of the 1905 Canadian Open, Cumming was responsible for inspiring an entire generation of young Canadian golf pros—including three Open champions: Charles and Albert Murray and Karl Keffer—and was nicknamed the "Dean" of Canadian professionals.

OPPOSITE The original clubhouse at the Toronto Golf Club, site of the 1905 and 1909 Canadian Open championships.

ABOVE The legendary Tommy Armour was a veteran not only of WWI but also of the Canadian Open when he won the 1927 title. He'd played in his first Canadian championship as an amateur—and tied for second with Charles Murray—at the 1920 Open.

OPPOSITE Karl Keffer was one of the pupils who bested his teacher, George Cumming. Keffer was 27 and the (Royal) Ottawa Golf Club professional when he won the 1909 Open over 30-year-old Cumming's Toronto Golf Club. In 1914, Keffer would again take the championship from Cumming on the Toronto club's new course on Dixie Road, west of the city.

Cumming, the Toronto Club's professional, claims the honours of the day by winning the open championship with a total score of 148 for the 36 holes. He came to Toronto from the Dumfries and Galloway Club in Scotland and can, as he has made very apparent, maintain the high prestige that attaches to the play of Scottish golfers on whatever links they may figure—let it be at St. Andrews or in Kabul.

The professionals, as was predicted in these columns, were certain claimants for the championship. Second on the list came Barrett, from the Lambton links, with a score of 151. Murray, the Royal Montreal pro, tied in 153 with Tait, from Erie, Penn. It is interesting to golfers to learn that Tait first coached Lieutenant Freddie Tait, the golfing son of the late Professor Tait, of Edinburgh University, and Lord Kelvin's distinguished contemporary in physics. Lieut. Tait held the Amateur championship of Scotland when he was killed in the Boer War while serving with his regiment, either the Gordons or the Black Watch, if memory serves right.

Mr. Douglas Laird is the first gentleman player mentioned in the championship list, his place being fourth. Already a champion in his university, which is Princeton, he is one of a band of young players who promise to reap a harvest of good records for the Toronto Club within the next few years. Mr. Laird heads the annual handicap list, both in the gross and net scores.

Many of those who were guests of the clubs followed the players during the early parts of the day. Unfortunately the excellent golfing weather that had prevailed throughout the tournament was slightly broken during the afternoon. Rain fell to an extent that prevented ladies and their friends watching the play of the saturated late starters. It did not, however, commence until the majority of the score cards had been handed in, and in no material way impaired the interest taken in the contests.

It looked at noon on Saturday, after the finish of the first 18 holes of the open championship, as if Charlie Murray, the professional of The Royal Montreal Golf Club, was going to win. He handed in a score for the first 18 of 74, which was better than Barrett by one stroke and Cumming by two.

Strange to say, the lowest morning score was handed in by Archie Kerr of the Toronto Club, who played with Oke, of

Ottawa, and who had not even entered the open class, but was playing for the handicap. He, with his handicap of two, led the handicap class easily. He made a 73 gross.

In the afternoon, Murray got into trouble on a couple of holes, which just made him score badly enough to put him out of the first two places; he took 79.

George Cumming ultimately took the title with a 76–72 148, three strokes better than Barrett of Lambton.

TORONTO GOLF CLUB

Kingston Road	YARDAGE: 5,125	PAR: N/A		DESIGNER: N/A

1905	FORMAT: 36 holes, 1 day	PURSE: $225, 1st place $60	
	DATE: July 1	WINNER: George Cumming, *Toronto Golf Club*	148
	FIELD: 22	RUNNER-UP: Percy Barrett, *Lambton Golf & Country Club*	151

1909	FORMAT: 72 holes, 2 days	PURSE: $265, 1st place $100	
	DATE: June 30/July 1	WINNER: Karl Keffer, *Toronto Golf Club*	309
	FIELD: 26	RUNNER-UP: George Cumming, *Toronto Golf Club*	312

Dixie Road	YARDAGE: 6,613	PAR: 73		DESIGNER: H.S. Colt

1914	FORMAT: 72 holes, 2 days	PURSE: $265, 1st place $100	
	DATE: August 13–14	WINNER: Karl Keffer, *Royal Ottawa Golf Club*	300
	FIELD: 32	RUNNER-UP: George Cumming, *Toronto Golf Club*	301

1921	FORMAT: 72 holes, 2 days	PURSE: $450, 1st place $250	
	DATE: August 1–2	WINNER: W.H. Trovinger, *Birmingham, Michigan*	293
	FIELD: 130	RUNNERS-UP: Mike Brady, *Detroit, Michigan*	296
		Bob MacDonald	296

1927	FORMAT: 72 holes (18, 18, 36), 3 days	PURSE: $1,320, 1st place $400	
	DATE: August 4–6	WINNER: Tommy Armour, *Washington, D.C.*	288
	FIELD: 61	RUNNER-UP: Macdonald Smith, *Long Island, New York*	289

NOTE: Where Par is marked with N/A is indicated as it was not a common practice to assign "par" for the course until following the War.

From its beginnings in the 19th century until the city began to encroach on the course, the Toronto Golf Club was located on Kingston Road (pictured here during the 1910 Canadian Ladies' Championship), in the east end of Toronto. In 1911, the club relocated west of the city to its current location on Dixie Road South, Mississauga, designed by one of the new breed of golf course architects, H. S. Colt.

Greater Ottawa

by KAREN HEWSON

The Open Golf Championship of Canada has been held in the Ottawa area on four occasions: twice at the Royal Ottawa Golf Club (1906 and 1911), at the Rivermead Club (1920) and at the Ottawa Hunt Club (1932). Charles Murray, professional of The Royal Montreal Golf Club, captured both titles contested at the Royal Ottawa, while J.D. Edgar repeated his 1919 victory when he came to Rivermead the next year and "Lighthorse" Harry Cooper won the 1932 Open over Ottawa Hunt.

There aren't many eyewitnesses left to draw on, but *Canadian Golfer* provides an excellent view of the 1920 championship with this report:

Douglas Edgar Repeats
Again Annexes Canadian Open Championship after a most exciting triple Play-off with Mr. T.D. Armour and Mr. C.R. Murray—Rivermead, Ottawa. Plays the host to Perfection—Remarkable Play of Several Young Amateurs one of the Features of a Thoroughly

ABOVE J. Douglas Edgar made his last appearance in the Canadian Open in 1920, where he won his second consecutive title. Edgar was killed the next year under mysterious circumstances in Atlanta.

OPPOSITE The clubhouse at the Royal Ottawa Golf Club. The Royal Ottawa moved to its current Alymer, Quebec location in 1901. The site of two Canadian Opens, the Ottawa club would receive the "Royal" prefix in 1911.

ABOVE The sixth hole at the Ottawa Hunt Club, host of the 1932 Canadian Open, where Harry Cooper captured his first of two titles. Cooper would tie for a 1938 playoff with Sam Snead, then tie the 18-hole playoff round. Snead finally wrestled the title from Cooper in the next nine-hole playoff.

Successful Championship—Governor-General of Canada an Interested Spectator of the Play, and Presents the Prizes.

The thirteenth open championship of Canada was staged on the Rivermead links at Ottawa on Thursday and Friday, August 26th and 27th (1920), and will go down in golfing history as one of the most memorable championships ever held in the Dominion.

The event was an outstanding one from the standpoint of completeness of detail, from the standpoint of the high-class list of entrants and from the standpoint, and this most important of all, of the play shown by a number of the younger contestants.

Then, of course, there was the thrill eventually of a triple play-off for premier honours, in which England was pitted against Scotland

and Canada against both; of an amateur contending against two professionals and the triumph once more of a representative of the latter class—a class which, all said and done, is largely responsible for the advancement of the game in this and every other golfing country.

The setting for the event was superb. The Rivermead course is ideally situated, with wonderful views of landscape and waterscape from a dozen different angles. And the officials of Rivermead for months before the championship had been busily engaged getting their house in order. Much intelligent work had been put on the bunkering and trapping of the course, whilst fairgreen and green had received most careful and expert attention.

The result was a splendid test of championship golf, and the many crack players in attendance were loud in their praises alike of

GOLF CHAMPIONSHIP

ROYAL CANADIAN GOLF ASSOCIATION

ADMISSION
$1.00

ABOVE Born in Troon, Scotland, a young Davie Black emigrated to Canada to take up a spot as golf pro at Montreal's Outremont Club. By 1911, he had moved to Ottawa's Rivermead Golf Club, where he gathered quite a following. Runner-up at the Canadian Open the same year, Black won the CPGA Championship on four occasions before he moved to Vancouver's Shaughnessy Golf and Country Club.

the links and the manner in which the event was conducted, from the first drive until the last putt.

There were in all 67 entries. This was hardly up to the total of 1919, when the last Open was held at Hamilton, but that event, it must be remembered, was preceded by the International match, and some of the U.S. amateurs and nearly all the Canadian team stayed over. With the exception of Mr. "Bobby" Jones, James Barnes and Leo Diegel, the field was just as representative, in fact from a Canadian standpoint even more representative.

Fresh from almost winning the big professional championship in the States (he was just nosed out in the finals by Jock Hutchinson), came Douglas Edgar, the former well-known English pro, now of Atlanta, Georgia, to defend the title he won in Hamilton last year with a sensational 278. With him was Louis Tellier, of Boston, the classy little French pro, who can always be depended upon to be in the seventies on any course. Then there were two new professional candidates for premier Canadian honours in George Ayton, of Regina, and J.B. Kinnear, of Winnipeg. These two Scottish players only arrived in Canada this spring and much interest centred in their first appearance here in a big event.

Davie Black, of Vancouver, where he a month or so ago won the Pacific Coast Championship, was on hand to make a bid for the laurel and as he was for many years at Rivermead he was looked upon as a dangerous contender indeed....

Then a decided international flavour was given to the championship by the presence of Mr. T.D. Armour, of Edinburgh, who only this summer won the French Open Amateur Championship, defeating in the finals the English Amateur champion, Mr. Cyril Tolley. Much was expected from this dashing Scottish amateur, and he did not disappoint his many admirers, who were very much with his play in his practice rounds before the tournament.

The officials decided to play the deciding round of the triple tie on Saturday at 12:30 p.m. One of the largest galleries that has ever found its way to the Rivermead golf course was present to witness the deciding round of the tournament...." (*Canadian Golfer*, VI 5, September 1920, 351–360).

Edgar won that playoff, and the rest, as they say, is history.

ROYAL OTTAWA GOLF CLUB

Aylmer, Quebec	YARDAGE: 6,310	PAR: N/A	DESIGNER: Tom Bendelow

1906
FORMAT: 36 holes, 1 day
DATE: July 7
FIELD: 24

PURSE: $225, 1st place, $70
WINNER: Charles Murray, *The Royal Montreal Golf Club* 170
RUNNERS-UP: George Cumming, *Toronto Golf Club* 171
Alex Robertson, *Victoria, B.C.* 171
*T.B. Reith, *Beaconsfield Golf Club* 171

1911
FORMAT: 72 holes, 2 days
DATE: July 7–8
FIELD: 24

PURSE: $265, 1st place $100
WINNER: Charles Murray, *The Royal Montreal Golf Club* 314
RUNNER-UP: Davie Black, *Rivermead Golf Club* 316

RIVERMEAD GOLF CLUB

Aylmer, Quebec	YARDAGE: 6,140	PAR: 72	DESIGNER: Kenneth Skodacek

1920
FORMAT: 72 holes, 2 days
DATE: August 26–27
FIELD: 67

PURSE: $600, 1st place $300
WINNER: J.D. Edgar, *Atlanta, Georgia* 298
RUNNERS-UP: Charles Murray, *The Royal Montreal Golf Club* 298
*Tommy Armour, *Edinburgh, Scotland* 298

Three-way tie decided in an 18-hole playoff the day after the event. They finished: Edgar, 73; Murray, 74; Armour, 75

OTTAWA HUNT CLUB

Ottawa, Ontario	YARDAGE: 6,770	PAR: 73	DESIGNER: Willie Park

1932
FORMAT: 72 holes, 3 days
DATE: July 7–9
FIELD: 120

PURSE: $1,465, 1st place $500
WINNER: Harry Cooper, *Chicago, Illinois* 290
RUNNER-UP: A.A. Watrous, *Birmingham, Michigan* 293

NOTE: Where Par is marked with N/A it was not a common practice to assign "par" for the course until following the War.

* Indicates Amateur competitor

Greater Montreal

by MARIO BRISEBOIS

Many people in golf believe the Canadian Opens in Quebec have always been held at The Royal Montreal Golf Club. Although the history of the Open in Quebec has indeed mainly been written at Royal Montreal, the cradle of golf in America, several very interesting chapters were written at other locations. In fact, 16 of the 25 Opens that have been held in *la belle province* since 1904 were presented elsewhere, including two at the Royal Ottawa Golf Club, located on the Quebec side of the Ottawa River. Interestingly, Charles Murray, professional at the Royal Montreal, won his two national titles at the Royal Ottawa Golf Club, in 1906 and 1911.

The only player to have won four Canadian Open titles, Leo Diegel captured his first at Mount Bruno in 1924 and his last at Kanawaki in 1929. On both occasions, Diegel triumphed over a Goliath: first Gene Sarazen and then Tommy Armour.

In the 1956 tournament, the Beaconsfield Golf Club was the site of a feat unique in the annals of the Open when Doug Sanders

ABOVE The Huots were the first family of Quebec golf. Three of the seven Huot brothers were professional golfers, and Jules was the most successful. He finished as low Canadian at the Open twice, including 1935, at Summerlea, and won the PGA Tour's General Brock Open in 1937. Left to right: Tony, Benoit, Roland, Rudolphe, Ulric, Maurice, Jules, Emmanuel.

OPPOSITE The Canadian Open travelled to the Montreal Municipal Golf Club in 1967 to help the city celebrate Expo 67. After four rounds, 1960 champion Art Wall Jr. and 1966 U.S. Open winner Billy Casper (pictured) were tied. In the 18-hole playoff, Casper prevailed, shooting a 65 to Wall's 69.

ABOVE Included in the field for the 1922 Canadian Open, held at Mount Bruno Golf Club, were five past champions—George Cumming, Charles Murray, Percy Barrett, Albert Murray and Karl Keffer—and eventual winner Al Watrous. Mount Bruno also hosted the 1924 Open, where Leo Diegel won the first of his record four Open titles.

became the only amateur to take the honours in 100 years and the first to win a national title against the pros since Johnny Goodman at the U.S. Open in 1933. At Laval-sur-le-Lac, in 1962, Charles Sifford almost became the first African-American player to win a PGA tournament, losing to Ted Kroll at the wire by only two strokes. Still, in 1962, there were two winners. Montreal journalist Larry O'Brien, a longtime friend of the RCGA, met a young player reputed to be full of talent. The young talent hired O'Brien as his secretary, then vice-president until his retirement in recent years. That young man was Jack Nicklaus.

In 1967, Canada's Centennial, the Open was held on a public golf course, the Montreal Municipal Golf Club, and was won by Billy Casper. Some were upset at the break with tradition in spite of the $200,000 purse put up by the Bronfman family. "For that much money, I would play in a shopping mall parking lot," said Chi Chi Rodriguez with his well-known flair.

Owner-player disputes are not limited to baseball, hockey and

football. In 1969, the Open at Pinegrove Country Club found itself in the middle of a major disagreement between the PGA and the players, which gave rise to the TPD (Tournament Players Division) Tour. As it was, the majority of the big names boycotted the event and Tommy Aaron took the win in a playoff against the then semi-retired Sam Snead, 57, who could have become the oldest champion in the history of the Open and of the PGA Tour had he won.

The 1971 Open, at Richelieu Valley, launched the beginning of a love affair between Lee Trevino and the Canadian Open, which he won three times. That year, Trevino won the Triple Crown for his wins at the American, British and Canadian Opens in the same year—a feat repeated 29 years later by Tiger Woods. The Merry Mexican had played the British Open wearing a Montreal Expos cap given to him by Gene Mauch, manager of the Montreal baseball team and an avid golfer.

So it's simply not true that over the years the home of the Open in Quebec was The Royal Montreal Golf Club...or anywhere else.

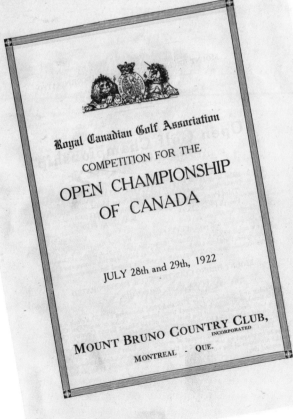

Royal Canadian Golf Association

COMPETITION FOR THE

OPEN CHAMPIONSHIP OF CANADA

JULY 28th and 29th, 1922

MOUNT BRUNO COUNTRY CLUB, INCORPORATED

MONTREAL - QUE.

MOUNT BRUNO GOLF CLUB

Montreal, Quebec   YARDAGE: 6,473   PAR: 70   DESIGNER: Willie Park Jr.

1922   FORMAT: 36 holes, 2 days   PURSE: $450, 1st place $250
        DATE: July 28–29   WINNER: A.A. Watrous, *Detroit, Michigan*   303
        FIELD: 85   RUNNER-UP: Tom Kerrigan, *Siwanoy, New York*   304

1924   FORMAT: 72 holes, 2 days   PURSE: $750, 1st place $400
        DATE: August 1–2   WINNER: Leo Diegel, *Detroit, Michigan*   285
        FIELD: 115   RUNNER-UP: Gene Sarazen, *Briarcliff, New York*   287

KANAWAKI GOLF CLUB

Kahnawake, Quebec   YARDAGE: 6,360   PAR: 70   DESIGNER: Albert Murray

1929   FORMAT: 72 holes, 2 days   PURSE: $1,325, 1st place $400
        DATE: July 25–27   WINNER: Leo Diegel, *Mount Vernon, New York*   274
        FIELD: 176   RUNNER-UP: Tommy Armour, *Detroit, Michigan*   277

SUMMERLEA GOLF AND COUNTRY CLUB

Vaudreuil-Dorion, Quebec   YARDAGE: 6,500   PAR: 70   DESIGNER: Geoffrey Cornish

1935   FORMAT: 72 holes, 3 days   PURSE: $1,270, 1st place $500
        DATE: August 29–31   WINNER: Gene Kunes, *Norristown, Pennsylvania*   280
        FIELD: 125   CUT: Low 60 and ties   RUNNER-UP: Victor Ghezzi, *Deal, New Jersey*   282

BEACONSFIELD GOLF CLUB

Pointe-Claire, Quebec   YARDAGE: 6,665   PAR: 72   DESIGNER: Stanley Thompson

1946   FORMAT: 72 holes, 4 days   PURSE: $9,000, 1st place $2,000
        DATE: June 27–30   WINNER: George Fazio, *Los Angeles, California*   278
        FIELD: 132   CUT: low 60 and ties   RUNNER-UP: Dick Metz, *Arkansas City, Arkansas*   278
                          18-hole playoff: Fazio, 70; Metz, 71

1956   FORMAT: 72 holes, 4 days   PURSE: $15,000, 1st place $2,400
        DATE: July 5–8   WINNER: *Doug Sanders, *Miami Beach, Florida*   273
        YARDAGE: 6,665   PAR: 72   RUNNER-UP: Dow Finsterwald, *Bedford Heights, Ohio*   273
        FIELD: 137   CUT: 63 players at 149   Playoff: One hole, won by Sanders. As Sanders was an
                          amateur, the first place purse went to runner-up Finsterwald

CLUB DE GOLF ISLESMERE

Montreal, Quebec   YARDAGE: 6,690   PAR: 72   DESIGNER: Willie Park Jr.

1959   FORMAT: 72 holes, 4 days   PURSE: $25,000, 1st place $3,500
        DATE: June 18–21   WINNER: Doug Ford, *Paradise, Florida*   276
        FIELD: N/A   RUNNERS-UP: Art Wall Jr., *Pocono Manor, Pennsylvania*   278
                          Dow Finsterwald, *Tequesta, Florida*   278
                          Bo Wininger, *Odessa, Texas*   278

NOTE: Where Par is marked with N/A it was not a common practice to assign "par" for the course until following the War.

* Indicates Amateur competitor

LE CLUB LAVAL-SUR-LE-LAC

Montreal, Quebec   YARDAGE: 6,555   PAR: 72   DESIGNER: Willie Park Jr.

1962   FORMAT: 72 holes, 4 days   PURSE: $30,000, 1st place $4,300
         DATE: July 26–29   WINNER: Ted Kroll, *Fort Lauderdale, Florida*   278
         FIELD: 195 entered   RUNNER-UP: Charles Sifford, *Los Angeles, California*   280
         CUT: 100 players at 156

PINEGROVE COUNTRY CLUB

St. Luc, Quebec   YARDAGE: 7,090   PAR: 71   DESIGNER: Howard Watson

1964   FORMAT: 72 holes, 4 days   PURSE: $50,000, 1st place $7,500
         DATE: July 30–August 2   WINNER: Kelvin Nagle, *Sydney, Australia*   277
         FIELD: 156   CUT: 152   RUNNER-UP: Arnold Palmer, *Laurel Valley, Pennsylvania*   279

1969   FORMAT: 72 holes, 4 days   PURSE: $125,000, 1st place $25,000
         DATE: July 24–27   WINNER: Tommy Aaron, *Callaway Gardens, Georgia*   275
         FIELD: N/A   RUNNER-UP: Sam Snead, *White Sulphur Springs, West Virginia* 275
         CUT: 79 players at 148   After 18-hole playoff: Aaron, 70; Snead, 72

MONTREAL MUNICIPAL GOLF CLUB

Montreal, Quebec   YARDAGE: 6,600   PAR: 71

1967   FORMAT: 72 holes, 4 days   PURSE: $200,000, 1st place $30,000
         DATE: June 29–July 2   WINNER: Billy Casper, *Peacock Gap, California*   279
         FIELD: 288 entries for 156 spots   RUNNER-UP: Art Wall Jr., *Honesdale, Pennsylvania*   279
         CUT: 81 at 147   After 18-hole playoff: Casper, 65; Wall, 69

RICHELIEU VALLEY GOLF CLUB

Ste-Julie de Vercheres, Quebec YARDAGE: 6,905 PAR: 72   DESIGNER: William & David Gordon

1971   FORMAT: 72 holes, 4 days   PURSE: $150,000, 1st place $30,000
         DATE: July 1–4   WINNER: Lee Trevino, *El Paso, Texas*   275
         FIELD: 146   RUNNER-UP: Art Wall Jr., *Honesdale, Pennsylvania*   275
         CUT: 78 players at 149   Playoff: Sudden-death, won by Trevino with a birdie

1973   FORMAT: 72 holes, 4 days   PURSE: $175,000, 1st place $35,000
         DATE: July 26–29   WINNER: Tom Weiskopf, *Columbus, Ohio*   278
         FIELD: 148   RUNNER-UP: Forrest Fezler, *Indian Wells, California*   280
         CUT: 82 players at four-over 148

ROYAL
NADIAN GOLF ASSOCIATION
CHAMPIONSHIPS
1929

THE CLUB HOUSE,
TORONTO

ABOVE Summerlea Golf and Country Club was the site of the 1935 Open, won by Gene Kunes.

RIGHT Among the Canadians entered in the field at the 1946 Canadian Open at Beaconsfield, were (left to right) Stan Leonard, Bob Gray, Gordie Brydson and Fred Wood. Leonard finished tied for second, which brought him the Rivermead Cup, while Brydson finished tied for seventh, Wood 16th and Gray 24th.

ABOVE LEFT George Fazio captured the 1946 Open in an 18-hole playoff, edging Dick Metz by a stroke, 70–71. Metz had birdied the final hole of regulation to force the playoff with Fazio (who later became a golf course architect, as did his nephew Tom). On the final hole of the playoff, Fazio needed a par to secure the victory. He did so with a 15-foot putt—but only after taking a one-stroke penalty when he hit into a flower bed.

ABOVE RIGHT Flag raising at the 1946 Open. Beaconsfield also hosted the 1956 Canadian Open, won by amateur Doug Sanders in the first instance of a sudden-death playoff to determine the winner. Sanders defeated Dow Finsterwald on the first hole of the playoff, making par to Finsterwald's bogey.

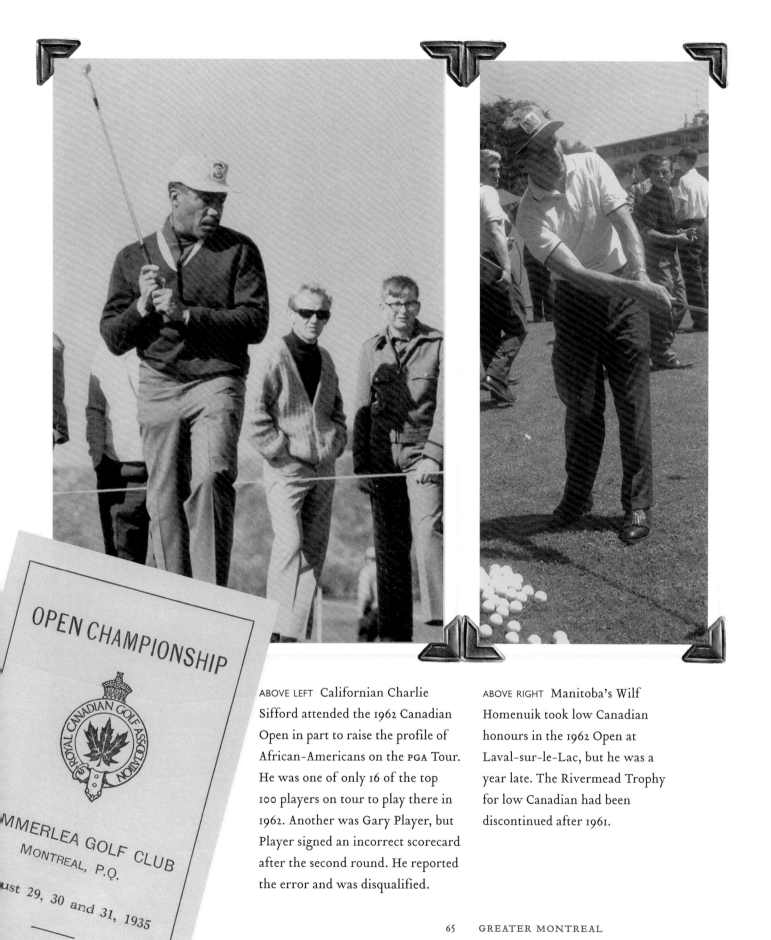

ABOVE LEFT Californian Charlie
Sifford attended the 1962 Canadian
Open in part to raise the profile of
African-Americans on the PGA Tour.
He was one of only 16 of the top
100 players on tour to play there in
1962. Another was Gary Player, but
Player signed an incorrect scorecard
after the second round. He reported
the error and was disqualified.

ABOVE RIGHT Manitoba's Wilf
Homenuik took low Canadian
honours in the 1962 Open at
Laval-sur-le-Lac, but he was a
year late. The Rivermead Trophy
for low Canadian had been
discontinued after 1961.

RIGHT Ex-Marine Ted Kroll edged Charlie Sifford by two strokes to win the 1962 Canadian Open, held at Le Club Laval-sur-le-Lac. Wilf Homenuik of Winnipeg finished as the low Canadian and tied for seventh, seven shots behind Kroll.

OPPOSITE The Richelieu Valley Golf Club hosted a pair of Canadian Opens in 1971 and 1973. Although he wasn't playing in his top form, Lee Trevino scrambled to shoot back-to-back 67s over the final two rounds in 1971 to match Art Wall Jr. In the playoff, Trevino won on the first hole with a birdie. In 1973, Tom Weiskopf captured the first of his two Canadian Opens, beating Forrest Fezler by two shots.

TOP The Kanawaki Golf Club played host to the Canadian Open in 1929, when Leo Diegel won the last of his four Open titles, beating his longtime rival Tommy Armour by three strokes.

LEFT AND OPPOSITE Pinegrove Country Club played host to the Canadian Open in 1964 and 1969. Australian Kel Nagle edged Arnold Palmer and Raymond Floyd at the 1964 Open to become the oldest player to win the title at the time. Five years later, Tommy Aaron fired a final-round 64 to force a playoff with Sam Snead. Aaron won the 18-hole playoff, beating Snead by two strokes, 70–72.

Lambton Golf & Country Club

by IAN CRUICKSHANK

Y ou can almost feel the ghosts as you pass down the long laneway that loops from Scarlet Road to the Lambton clubhouse. Over the past century, Harry Vardon, George Lyon, Walter Hagen and Sam Snead are just some of the legends who have travelled along this road to tee it up at Lambton. The Toronto club has hosted dozens of important championships over the years, but none more important than its four Canadian Opens.

Lambton's origins are due to the vision of a single man, an entrepreneurial whirlwind named Albert William Austin. As President of the Dominion Bank and the Consumers' Gas Company, Austin was one of the country's corporate movers and shakers. But golf was his lasting legacy.

Austin realized that the newly-invented rubber core ball was about to change the game forever, and so, in the days when 4,000 yards constituted a long ball course, he commissioned a 6,000-yard monster—a true championship test, with a matching, state-of-the-art clubhouse.

ABOVE Aerial shot of the Lambton Golf and Country Club from the 1941 Canadian Open, won by Sam Snead. Lambton not only hosted the championship on four occasions, but also its own professional, Percy Barrett, won the title on his home course in 1907.

OPPOSITE Lambton Golf and Country Club clubhouse, circa 1910.

ABOVE LEFT Sam Snead won three Canadian Open titles in four years, the last at the 1941 championship, at Lambton, in an 18-hole playoff with the 1939 champion, Harold McSpaden.

ABOVE RIGHT Lambton's fourth hole remains exactly as it was played in 1907 and every year since.

Austin found his perfect piece of golfing property at Lambton Mills, a 150-acre stretch of farm and river land at the western edge of Toronto. Incorporated in July of 1902, within a year the new club's course and clubhouse were open and filled with members. Austin was such a super salesman that he convinced nearly a third of the membership of the established Rosedale Golf Club to follow him to Lambton. Included in that number was George Lyon, then setting a score of amateur records that may never be bettered. It was as a Lambton member that Lyon captured the gold medal in golf at the 1904 Olympic Games.

Lambton's first professional was Percy Barrett from England. A protégé of six-time British Open winner Harry Vardon, the home pro promptly won the title when Lambton hosted its first Open in 1907. Three years later, Daniel Kenny, a Scotsman playing out of Buffalo, crossed the border to win the 1910 Open at Lambton. When the Open returned to the club in 1925, PGA champion Leo Diegel held off Walter Hagen to win his second consecutive Canadian title. Then Sam Snead sealed his third Open championship by slamming a 375-yard drive on

LAMBTON GOLF AND COUNTRY CLUB

Toronto, Ontario   YARDAGE: 6,604   PAR: 71   DESIGNER: Willie Dunn

1907 FORMAT: 72 holes, 2 days
DATE: July 5–6
FIELD: 24

PURSE: $245, 1st place $80
WINNER: Percy Barrett, *Lambton Golf & Country Club*   306
RUNNER-UP: George Cumming, *Toronto Golf Club*   308

Barrett was the first professional to win the Canadian Open over his home course

1910 FORMAT: 72 holes, 2 days
DATE: July 7–8
FIELD: 26

PURSE: $265, 1st place $100
WINNER: Daniel Kenny, *Buffalo, New York*   303
RUNNER-UP: *George S. Lyon, *Lambton Golf & Country Club* 307

1925 FORMAT: 72 holes, 3 days
DATE: July 30–August 1
FIELD: 165
CUT: players at 164 or better after 36 holes

PURSE: $900, 1st place $500
WINNER: Leo Diegel, *Detroit, Michigan*   295
RUNNER-UP: Mike Brady, *Mamaroneck, New York*   297

1941 FORMAT: 72 holes, 3 days
DATE: August 7–9
FIELD: 131
CUT: players with 151 or better after 36 holes

PURSE: $3,000, 1st place $1,000
WINNER: Sam Snead, *Shawnee-on-Delaware, Pennsylvania* 274
RUNNER-UP: Bob Gray, *Scarboro Golf & Country Club*   276

Lambton's 10th hole, making an eagle to take the lead for good in 1941.

The architectural legacy behind Lambton's two golf courses—its 18-hole layout and nine-hole valley course—is nearly as impressive as its tournament history. The original course was laid out by Scotsman Willie Dunn, whose plan included a 750-yard par-six. Dunn's musclebound master plan was changed by the club, with suggestions from George Lyon and Scottish American architect Tom Bendelow. Later, Donald Ross, then Stanley Thompson and more recently Graham Cooke have put their imprints on the course.

In 2001, the club opened a new clubhouse that is dotted with reminders of the club's sterling golfing past. A stirring, full-length painting of George Lyon dominates the foyer; dozens of black-and-white photos featuring everyone from Harry Vardon (who played Lambton in 1913) to Walter Hagen are sprinkled throughout, and a handsome bronze plaque with the names and dates of its Canadian Open and Canadian Amateur winners is affixed to the pro shop—just another reminder of Lambton's leading place in Canadian golf history.

NOTE: Where Par is marked with N/A it was not a common practice to assign "par" for the course until following the War.

* Indicates Amateur competitor

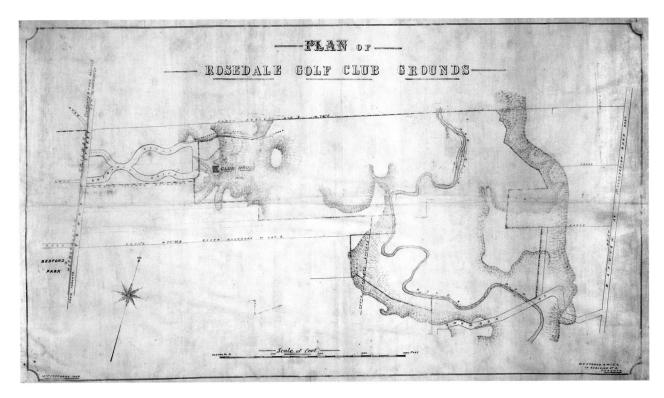

Greater Toronto

by JOHN GORDON

Revisiting the Canadian Opens mentioned here is akin to strolling through a couple of Halls of Fame: One for players and another for the architects and the projects they made. Though neither category should necessarily be ranked in chronological order, consider the 1912 Open at the Rosedale Golf Club.

Until then, our Open had been contested largely by golfers from this country, whether native-born or immigrant professionals from Scotland, England and Ireland. But in 1912 Rosedale welcomed "Long" Jim Barnes, two-time U.S. Open winner Alex Smith and a teenager named Walter Hagen. Won by George Sargent, the former head professional at Royal Ottawa, it was a portent of things to come—a deluge of talent from south of the border. Indeed, the next winner at Rosedale would be Leo Diegel, the arms-out putter who registered the third of his total of four Canadian Open victories on the Donald Ross–designed Toronto course in 1928.

Arguably as talented as Ross, though certainly not as acknowledged, Toronto-born architect Stanley Thompson contributed

ABOVE The Rosedale Golf Club hosted the Canadian Open twice, in 1912 and 1928. Relocated in 1909, this plan shows the layout of the current property when it was purchased and demonstrates (if dimly) how the river crisscrossed the valley. Although the course was initially laid out by Tom Bendelow, it was implemented by the club's professional, W. J. Lock. It was this course that was played in the 1912 Open.

OPPOSITE The 18th green at Angus Glen is ringed with spectators for the exciting three-way playoff on the Sunday of the 2002 Bell Canadian Open.

ABOVE Left to right; Charles Murray, Billy Bell, Frank Freeman, Karl Keffer, Albert Murray, Willie Freeman and George Cumming strike a pose to show a group of the Canadian contingent— and Cumming's pupils—at the 1912 Open. This tournament at Rosedale also marked the professional debut of 19-year-old Walter Hagen.

three courses covered in this chapter. A co-founder with Ross of the American Society of Golf Course Architects, the colourful Thompson laid out St. Andrews (which no longer exists at its location near the present-day Toronto intersection of Highway 401 and Yonge Street), Thornhill Country Club in Toronto, as well as St. George's Golf and Country Club. Thompson would not have been disappointed in the players who emerged victorious from his courses: Lawson Little, in 1936, and Harry Cooper, in 1937, added to their impressive resumes at St. Andrews; and Byron Nelson won his 11th consecutive tournament—one PGA Tour record that may stand forever—at Thornhill in 1945.

Willie Park Jr., twice winner of the Open in his native Scotland, was also a prolific architect on both sides of the Atlantic. Included in his several Canadian designs was the Weston Golf and Country Club, where, in 1955, a struggling Tour rookie named Arnold Palmer

would win his first pro tournament. It would prove to be the springboard for a monumental career.

Not to be forgotten are Herbert Strong, designer of Lakeview, just west of Toronto, where C.W. Hackney (1923) and the famed Silver Scot, Tommy Armour (1934), would win titles. Most recently, John Rollins claimed the 2002 Open title at Angus Glen, laid out by Thompson disciple Doug Carrick.

Like the trophies and the reputations of these Open winners, the courses that have witnessed Canadian golf history have become burnished over time. Bright with memories, they, and the men responsible for designing and building them, should be equally cherished.

ABOVE LEFT Toronto's St. Andrews Golf Club hosted the Open in 1936 and 1937— the only place to hold back-to-back Opens until the creation of Glen Abbey—before it felt the impact of the growth of the city and was plowed under to create Highway 401.

ABOVE RIGHT Left to right, Gene Sarazen, Tommy Armour and Walter Hagen, three of the most powerful names in golf of the time, at Lakeview Golf Club, 1934. Armour would win the championship that year, his third victory, while Hagen was the 1931 champion. Sarazen never took the Canadian Open but came close as runner-up in 1924 and 1926.

ROSEDALE GOLF CLUB

Toronto, Ontario   DESIGNERS: Tom Bendelow / Donald Ross

1912 FORMAT: 72 holes, 2 days   PURSE: $265, 1st place $100
DATE: August 8–9   WINNER: George Sargent, *Washington, DC*   299
YARDAGE: 5,275 PAR: 67   RUNNER-UP: Jim Barnes, *Tacoma, Washington*   302
FIELD: 30

1928 FORMAT: 72 holes, 3 days   PURSE: $1,320, 1st place $400
DATE: July 26–28   WINNER: Leo Diegel, *Mount Vernon, New York*   282
YARDAGE: 6,240 PAR: 72   RUNNERS-UP: Archie Compston, *Great Britain*   284
                                          Walter Hagen, *New York, New York*   284
FIELD: 144   CUT: 160   Macdonald Smith, *Long Island, New York*   284

LAKEVIEW GOLF CLUB

Mississauga, Ontario   YARDAGE: 6,263   PAR: 70   DESIGNER: Herbert Strong

1923 FORMAT: 72 holes, 2 days   PURSE: $580, 1st place $350
DATE: August 3–4   WINNER: C.W. Hackney, *Atlantic City, New Jersey*   295
FIELD: 139   CUT: 68 players at 175   RUNNER-UP: Tom Kerrigan, *Siwanoy, New York*   300
Headlights used for first day: eliminated all high scores (20 back of first 10)

1934 FORMAT: 72 holes, 3 days   PURSE: $1,465, 1st place $500
DATE: August 2–4   WINNER: Tommy Armour, *Chicago, Illinois*   287
FIELD: 159   CUT: low 60 and ties   RUNNER-UP: Ky Laffoon, *Denver, Colorado*   289

ST. ANDREWS GOLF CLUB

Toronto, Ontario   YARDAGE: 6,625   PAR: 70   DESIGNER: Stanley Thompson

1936 FORMAT: 72 holes, 3 days   PURSE: $3,000, 1st place $1,000
DATE: September 10–12   WINNER: Lawson Little, *Chicago, Illinois*   271
FIELD: 189   RUNNER-UP: Jimmy Thompson, *Shawnee, Pennsylvania* 279

1937 FORMAT: 72 holes, 3 days   PURSE: $3,200, 1st place, $1,000
DATE: September 9–11   WINNER: Harry Cooper, *Chicopee, Massachusetts*   285
FIELD: 169   RUNNER-UP: Ralph Guldahl, *Chicago, Illinois*   287

NOTE: Where Par is marked with N/A it was not a common practice to assign "par" for the course until following the War.

THORNHILL COUNTRY CLUB

Toronto, Ontario   YARDAGE: 6,317   PAR: 70   DESIGNER: Stanley Thompson

1945   FORMAT: 72, 3 days   PURSE: $10,000, 1st place $2,000
      DATE: August 2–4   WINNER: Byron Nelson, *Toledo, Ohio*   280
      FIELD: 150   RUNNER-UP: Hermann Barron, *White Plains, New York*   284
      CUT: low 60 and ties at 158

WESTON GOLF AND COUNTRY CLUB

Toronto, Ontario   YARDAGE: 6,428   PAR: 72   DESIGNER: Willie Park Jr.

1955   FORMAT: 72 holes, 4 days   PURSE: $15,000
      DATE: August 15–20   WINNER: Arnold Palmer, *Latrobe, Pennsylvania*   265
      FIELD: 150   RUNNER-UP: Jack Burke, *Klamesha Lake, New York*   269
      CUT: low 60 and ties at 143

ANGUS GLEN GOLF CLUB

South Course, Markham, Ontario   YARDAGE: 7,372   PAR: 72   DESIGNER: Doug Carrick

2002   FORMAT: 72 holes, 4 days   PURSE: $4 million, 1st place $720,000
      DATE: September 2–8   WINNER: John Rollins, *Richmond, Virginia*   272
      FIELD: 156   RUNNERS-UP: Neal Lancaster, *Smithfield, North Carolina*   272
      CUT: 82 players at 143   Justin Leonard, *Dallas, Texas*   272
                           Playoff: one extra hole

In 1919, Rosedale hired the famous Donald Ross to redesign Bendelow's and Lock's work. The result replaced Bendelow's flat greens with Ross's characteristic undulations.

Byron Nelson holes out a long putt for a birdie at the last hole of the
Thornhill Country Club to win the 1945 Open Championship with a
total of 280, and to capture his 11th consecutive PGA Tour title.

LEFT After capturing the 1955 Canadian Open championship, his first PGA Tour victory, Arnold Palmer demonstrates his reverse C finish—not the finishing position for which Arnie was to become famous—for the instruction section of *Canadian Sport Monthly* magazine.

ABOVE Little-known John Rollins was ecstatic when he defeated multiple winner Justin Leonard and journeyman Neal Lancaster in a three-way playoff for the 2002 Bell Canadian Open championship at Angus Glen. Lancaster had led throughout the day but faltered on the second-last hole, ending up in the playoff with Rollins and Leonard.

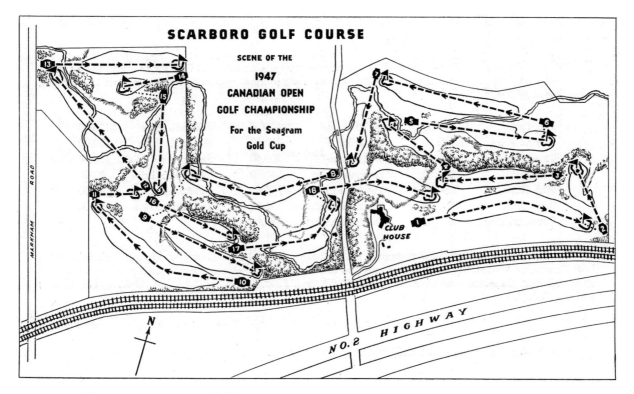

Scarboro Golf & Country Club

DAVE PERKINS

The four Canadian Opens played at the Scarboro Golf and Country Club are so far away—yet they were so close.

Three championships were decided by one stroke and the only time the margin was two shots was when Bobby Locke defeated Ed "Porky" Oliver in 1947. The margin was that wide only because a radio reporter fed Locke incorrect information that led to his gambling for—and making—a late birdie he didn't need.

There will be no more Opens at Scarboro, given its undaunting length—at least by modern standards—and its lack of available land for tent cities and other modern professional trappings. But even though its last Open was played more than 40 years ago, the hilly 18 crisscrossing Highland Creek—the only surviving course in Canada designed by the legendary A.W. Tillinghast—has already provided a fat chapter of historical lore.

The first Open played there went to a Monday playoff. In 1940, Sunday sports in Toronto were still two decades away. After Sam Snead frittered away a final-round lead on Saturday, setting up an

ABOVE When Scarboro hosted the 1947 Open, the tournament was quite a different sort of spectacle than it had been in 1940. This was the first time weekly tickets were sold, and they were offered in advance of the tournament. There was a PGA golf clinic on Tuesday afternoon, and the greens and tees were roped off so that everyone could have a decent view without crowding the bunkers and greens.

OPPOSITE The original 18 holes at Scarboro were laid out in 1912, but in 1924 the club hired A.W. Tillinghast to remodel 11 of the 18 holes. Highland Creek winds its way through the course and comes into play on 12 holes.

SCARBORO GOLF AND COUNTRY CLUB

By the time the last Canadian Open at the Scarboro Golf and Country Club was played in 1963, golf tournaments were beginning to look more like they do today. Scoreboards were dotted around the course to assist the ever-growing numbers of spectators, companies began to take advantage of visual advertising and spectators would enjoy a day on the golf course along with watching great golf. The 1963 tournament ended with Doug Ford edging Al Geiberger by a stroke to capture his second Canadian Open.

18-hole showdown with Harold "Jug" McSpaden, the free day and an economic opportunity presented themselves nicely. Snead spent the off day playing a paid exhibition match with Ralph Guldahl in Niagara Falls. In the playoff, Snead got behind early, then drove the green at the tactical 294-yard par-four 15th hole and made birdie to tie. Tied at the 18th, McSpaden somehow left a two-foot par putt short to finish 72 to Snead's par round of 71. McSpaden needn't have felt too badly; both men had agreed to split first and second money ($1,200 and $700). And Snead did win those 81 other PGA Tour tournaments.

By 1947, the second Open at Scarboro, local eyes were pasted on club professional Bob Gray, who held the job at Scarboro for more than 30 years, until he passed away in 1967. Gray, who had finished second to Snead in the Open at Toronto's Lambton in 1941, drew the largest galleries all four days—and Scarboro sold a whopping 3,478 final-round admissions, at the wallet-busting price of $1.50 each.

In an account that foreshadows what Mike Weir would feel at Hamilton in 2003, a local newspaper summed up the pressure as

Gray contended: "Gray was on the spot all the way around. Every time he moved, someone in the gallery reminded him that he was the lone Canadian leader. 'You can do it. We know you can,' well-wishers shouted to him as he walked along between shots. You could almost see his big shoulders sagging with the load he carried."

Gray finished tied for fifth at 277 after Locke posted a then Open record of 268. The South African, one of the first great international players, held a one-shot lead over Oliver, despite Oliver blasting into the cup for birdie after hitting his ball onto the muddy bank of the creek at the par-three fourth hole. At the 17th tee, a radio reporter who couldn't add shouted to Locke that a 269 had been posted, causing Locke to pull his driver on the dogleg 373-yard par-four. He boomed his tee shot over the trees at the corner within 20 yards of the green and made a birdie. A routine par at the 18th nursed the eventual winning margin. Locke's scorecard—signed Bobby Locke, South Africa—remains a treasured keepsake at the club today.

Another one-shot win was provided in 1953 when Dave Douglas came from four shots behind in the final day to defeat journeyman

ABOVE The par-four 18th at Scarboro Golf and Country Club has seen many memorable moments in the four Canadian Opens played there, including the third birdie in a row by Dave Douglas, who went on to win the 1953 Open by a single stroke over Wally Ulrich.

ABOVE With his win at Scarboro in 1947, Bobby Locke of South Africa became the first non–North American–based winner of the Canadian Open. Locke fired four rounds in the 60s to finish at 16-under-par, two strokes better than American "Porky" Oliver. After the prizes were presented, Locke was given a standing ovation and then hoisted to the shoulders of his countrymen who were now residents of Canada.

OPPOSITE Three-time Canadian Open champion Sam Snead, pictured here (second from left) at a charity function in Toronto, won his second Open title at Scarboro in 1940. Slammin' Sammy defeated 1939 winner Harold McSpaden in an 18-hole playoff.

Wally Ulrich. Douglas birdied the first three and the last three holes and shot a six-under 65, but needed Ulrich to double-bogey the 15th, then leave a 12-foot par putt hanging on the lip to finish one shot behind. The two men played together as their wives perched together on the Scarboro clubhouse veranda, nervously smoking cigarettes. They were both superstitious and thought they'd bring their men bad luck by watching them play.

The final Scarboro Open was held in 1963. Doug Ford was leading by two strokes after the second round and three after the third on a course stretched out by some new tees (now mostly gone) to 6,752 yards. Al Geiberger, famous for once shooting 59, posted an early 65, including 30 on the back nine, and sat for an hour on the veranda, sipping lemonade and watching a scoreboard show Ford's lead slip away. Ford was tied at the 17th tee but played safe with a 4-iron off the tee. His wedge left him 18 feet, but he made the putt to go a shot ahead. Geiberger then watched as a ball arrived at the 18th green, six feet from the hole. "That'll be Doug," Geiberger announced of the approach shot. It was. Two routine putts later, Ford was one more one-stroke winner.

SCARBORO GOLF AND COUNTRY CLUB

Toronto, Ontario   DESIGNER: A.W. Tillinghast

1940 FORMAT: 72 holes, 3 days
DATE: August 15–17
YARDAGE: 6,554 PAR 71
FIELD: 129

PURSE: $3,000, 1st place $1,000
WINNER: Sam Snead, *Shawnee-on-Delaware, Pennsylvania* 281
RUNNER-UP: Harold "Jug" McSpaden, *Winchester, Massachusetts* 281
Playoff: 18 holes, Snead 71, McSpaden 72

1947 FORMAT: 72 holes, 4 days
DATE: July 16–19
YARDAGE: 6,554 PAR 71
FIELD: 165   CUT: 78 players at 155

PURSE: $10,000, 1st place $2,000
WINNER: Bobby Locke, *South Africa* 268
RUNNER-UP: Ed Oliver, *Wilmington, Delaware* 270

1953 FORMAT: 72 holes, 4 days
DATE: July 8–11
YARDAGE: 6,469 PAR 71
FIELD: 175   CUT: 64 players at 149

PURSE: $15,000, 1st place $3,000
WINNER: Dave Douglas, *Newark, Delaware* 273
RUNNER-UP: Wally Ulrich, *St. Paul, Minnesota* 274

1963 FORMAT: 72 holes, 4 days
DATE: July 3–6
YARDAGE: 6,752 PAR 71
FIELD: 156   CUT: 86 players at 150

PURSE: $50,000, 1st place $9,000
WINNER: Doug Ford, *New York, New York* 280
RUNNER-UP: Al Geiberger, *Carlton Oaks, California* 281

Riverside Country Club

by PETER MCGUIRE

ack in 1992, New Brunswick golf fans—more specifically, those at the Riverside Country Club, on the outskirts of Canada's oldest incorporated city, Saint John—got a first-hand glimpse of a future PGA Tour star when Mike Weir went shot for shot against local boy Darren Ritchie before coming up two shots short against the scrappy 27-year-old from Hampton. It was the first time that a player east of Quebec would walk away as the Canadian men's amateur champion. It didn't deter Weir though. The left-hander from Bright's Grove, Ontario, turned professional shortly after and began blazing a trail that would see him become Canada's first male golfer to win a major by capturing the 2003 Masters title.

But 64 years before that, some of the greatest players of the day had strolled the grounds at the same Donald Ross-designed layout when the 1939 Canadian Open was staged in the Maritimes for the first and only time. The man responsible for landing such a monumental event was one of the club's most distinguished members, Percy W. Thomson, a shipping magnate (and the brother of five-time

ABOVE In 1939, the Canadian Open was held for the first and only time in the Maritimes, at Riverside Country Club in Saint John, New Brunswick. Played a few weeks before the outbreak of the Second World War, American "Jug" McSpaden captured the title by five strokes over Ralph Guldahl.

OPPOSITE Riverside's 18th green, overlooking the Saint John River, has been the scene of many exciting finishes including several Canadian Amateur Championships like the one shown here in 1963.

Canadian women's champion Mabel Thomson) who had fallen in love with the game.

After Thompson footed the bill for a major overhaul of the course and natural maturation, Riverside would soon gain a reputation as one of Canada's premier challenges. Thomson invited four of the top touring professionals—Horton Smith, Jimmy Thomson, Lawson Little and Harry Cooper—to play an exhibition match at Riverside. The quartet was so impressed that they suggested that the Royal Canadian Golf Association stage the Canadian Open there. A short time later, it was announced that Riverside would be the site of the 1939 Canadian Open.

Harold "Jug" McSpaden, of Winchester, Massachusetts, put on a sparkling display that helped earn him and his close friend, the legendary Byron Nelson, the co-moniker of the "Gold Dust Twins" for their domination of the pro game. McSpaden set the tone early, displaying a

32ND CANADIAN OPEN GOLF CHAMPIONSHIP

RIVERSIDE
Golf and Country Club
SAINT JOHN NEW BRUNSWICK

Thursday, Friday, Saturday, August 17th - 18th - 19th, 1939

Official Program
★ ★ ★
25 cents

superb touch that translated into a course-record 67 for a two-stroke lead over three golfers—including pre-tournament favourite Ralph Guldahl of New Jersey—and continued to demonstrate his mastery of the game, especially around the greens, as he cruised to a five-stroke victory with a total score of two-over 282 in the 72-hole tournament to collect the first-place prize of $1,000. The breathtaking scenic layout overlooking the Kennebecasis River blended beautifully with McSpaden's fine play, as the gallery of several thousand on the final day would attest.

McSpaden would go on to be named to a number of Ryder Cup teams during the war years but unfortunately for him was denied the chance to compete because of the conflict. Instead, McSpaden and his Ryder Cup teammates—who included Gene Sarazen, Byron Nelson, Sam Snead and Ben Hogan—played charity exhibition matches against the likes of Walter Hagen and the great Bobby Jones to raise funds for such causes as the American Red Cross and the USO.

Meanwhile, the setting for McSpaden's 1939 Canadian Open triumph would go on to host a number of high-profile events, such as the Canadian Amateur in 1949 (Dick Chapman), 1963 (Nick Weslock), 1975 (Jim Nelford) and 1992 (Darren Ritchie); the CPGA Championship in 1947 (Rudolphe Huot); the 1948 Canadian Ladies' Open (Grace Lenzcyk); the 1995 Canadian Junior Championship (Jesse Collinson); and the 2002 Canadian Senior Ladies' Championship (Allison Murdoch).

All such champions are rightfully inscribed in the history of New Brunswick's most celebrated club, but perhaps it is still McSpaden who heads that formidable list.

RIVERSIDE COUNTRY CLUB

Saint John, New Brunswick YARDAGE: 6,231   PAR: 70   DESIGNER: Donald Ross

1939   FORMAT: 72 holes, 3 days   PURSE: $3,000, 1st place $1,000
          DATE: August 17–19   WINNER: Harold "Jug" McSpaden, *Winchester, Massachusetts* 282
          FIELD: 84   RUNNER-UP: Ralph Guldahl, *Madison, New Jersey*   287

Hamilton Golf & Country Club

by GARRY MCKAY

The Canadian Open has only come to the Hamilton Golf and Country Club three times in the event's 100-year history. But those three occasions were filled with enough drama, excitement and record-breaking performances for a century. Founded in 1894, the Hamilton G&CC moved to its third home, in the village of Ancaster, in 1916. Three years later, in 1919, the H.S. Colt-designed course hosted its first Canadian Open. A strong contingent of American players, including Francis Ouimet and a 17-year-old amateur star from Atlanta, Bobby Jones, came to Hamilton to play in a series of matches against the top Canadians and then stayed for the Open the following week.

The tournament turned out to be a one-man show, however. J. Douglas Edgar, an Englishman transplanted to Atlanta, Georgia, demolished the field by shooting a then world record 72–71–69–66–278 to win by an astounding 16 strokes, a margin of victory that has stood as the Canadian Open and PGA Tour record for more than 84 years. Jones, who never played in another Canadian Open in his

ABOVE One of the biggest attractions at the 1930 Canadian Open was Walter Hagen, shown here leaving the 18th green. Hagen finished in sixth place at 280, four strokes out of the playoff between Tommy Armour and Leo Diegel.

OPPOSITE Play on the third green at the Hamilton Golf and Country Club, where J. Douglas Edgar won the first of his consecutive titles. The Hamilton club had only recently relocated to its Ancaster home when it hosted the 1919 Canadian Open. Designed by H.S. Colt, the original 18 holes at this course have stood the test of time, with scores of 278 in 1919 and 272 in 2003—84 years later.

ABOVE LEFT Bobby Jones was but a youth when he began taking the golf world by storm, a condition that continued for another decade before he retired from competitive golf, and a mere 17 when he came to Canada to take part in the international matches between Canada and the United States held at Hamilton before the Canadian Open in 1919. He played well, but he couldn't compete with J. D. Edgar's record score of 278 and finished in second place.

legendary career, was tied for second with Jim Barnes of St. Louis and Karl Keffer of Ottawa, the defending champion.

The championship returned to the Hamilton club in 1930 for what might have then been the longest tournament in Canadian Open history. It began on a Friday and didn't end until the following Wednesday. Tommy Armour, the Silver Scot, won the second of his three Canadian Opens titles in a playoff with Leo Diegel, the defending and two-time champion. After playing 36 holes on Friday, the tournament was scheduled to end with 36 on Saturday. Armour came from five strokes off the pace with a final-round, course-record-setting 64 to tie Diegel. Tournament golf wasn't allowed on Sunday, and Armour was scheduled to be in Detroit on Monday. The players agreed to come back to Hamilton on Wednesday for a 36-hole

playoff that Armour won by shooting 69–69–138 to Diegel's 69–72–141 to take home the $500 first prize.

When the RCGA decided to bring the 2003 Bell Canadian Open to Hamilton after an absence of 73 years, a lot of eyebrows were raised. After all, the course, built in 1916, would be the oldest the Open had ever been played on. It became a test of whether older courses could stand up to modern technology and the Hamilton Golf and Country Club passed. Bob Tway won the title in a three-hole playoff with Brad Faxon, but Tway's winning score of 272 (eight-under) was the highest relative to par of any event on the PGA Tour outside the majors that year. And the players loved the look, the feel and the challenge of playing an historic old course.

ABOVE The 1930 Canadian Open at Hamilton was another stellar tournament. Tommy Armour blazed his way around the final 18 holes of regulation play— shooting a 64. When four-time champion Leo Diegel and Armour went to a 36-hole playoff to decide the title, Armour shot 138 (69–69) to defeat Diegel by three strokes.

ABOVE Canada's first Masters champion, Mike Weir, came to the 2003 Open as both the hometown favourite and a player with a better than average shot at the title. Hamilton was a course he had played competitively in the provincial amateur championship, and he was at the top of his game. Mike wasn't to win this Open, finishing tied for 10th, but he gave it a valiant effort.

OPPOSITE It took three playoff holes, but 44-year-old Bob Tway (left) finally defeated Brad Faxon to capture the 2003 Bell Canadian Open, and in the process became the oldest player to win the tournament, surpassing 1964 champion Kel Nagle by a year. Faced with a 25-foot putt for par on the 72nd hole, Tway almost didn't

get to that playoff. Afterwards, Tway had nothing but good things to say about the 87-year-old Hamilton layout. "I don't know what it was about those guys who built golf courses in the early 1900s, but they really knew what they were doing. This is a very special place."

HAMILTON GOLF AND COUNTRY CLUB

Ancaster, Ontario   DESIGNER: H.S. Colt

1919   FORMAT: 72 holes, 2 days
DATE: July 29–30
YARDAGE: 6,470   PAR: 70
FIELD: 88   CUT: 54 players at 169

PURSE: $435, 1st place $200
WINNER: J. Douglas Edgar, *Atlanta, Georgia*   278
RUNNERS-UP: James Barnes, *St. Louis, Missouri*   294
     Bobby Jones, *Atlanta, Georgia*   294
     Karl Keffer, *Royal Ottawa Golf Club*   294

1930   FORMAT: 72 holes, 3 days
DATE: July 24–26
YARDAGE: 6,470   PAR: 70
FIELD: 169   CUT: 43 players at 155

PURSE: $1,475, 1st place $500
WINNER: Tommy Armour, *Detroit, Michigan*   277
RUNNER-UP: Leo Diegel, *Agua Caliente, Mexico*   277
After 18-hole playoff: Armour, 138; Diegel, 141

2003   FORMAT: 72 holes, 4 days
DATE: September 1–7
YARDAGE: 6,946   PAR: 70
FIELD: 156   CUT: 81 players at 143

PURSE: $4.2 million, 1st place $756,000
WINNER: Bob Tway, *Oklahoma City, Oklahoma*   272
RUNNER-UP: Brad Faxon, *Barrington, Rhode Island*   272
Playoff: Sudden-death, went to third extra hole

Mississaugua Golf & Country Club

by IAN HUTCHINSON

There is no easy way to define the perfect setting for golf unless it's by personal taste—and Tom Jenkins seemed to find what he was looking for as he was about to defend his 2000 AT&T Canada Senior Open championship. The following year, the venue was the Mississaugua Golf and Country Club. Yards away from the busy Queen Elizabeth Way west of Toronto, stately trees, rolling topography and scenic vistas along the Credit River characterize a round at this six-time host to the Canadian Open. "This is an old-style golf course," said an enthused Jenkins, whose 10 appearances in the Canadian Open had not included a stop at Mississaugua. "All golf courses are basically the same. Every golf course has tee boxes, fairways and greens you have to hit. The thing about old-style golf courses is the atmosphere. You don't have homes all around and the trees are magnificent. It gives you a feeling of what golf is supposed to be."

What golf is supposed to be has intangible qualities. While American stars such as Walter Hagen and Slammin' Sammy Snead

ABOVE Legends from the 1965 Canadian Open at the Mississaugua G&CC include Arnold Palmer hitching a ride up the Credit River with two boys in a canoe, Gary Player and Jack Nicklaus bombing the canoe with rocks, and Player mimicking Palmer's swing on the 13th tee. Here Nicklaus searches for his ball on the 12th.

OPPOSITE The Mississaugua Golf and Country Club has hosted six Canadian Opens, and the 18th hole, shown here in 1965, was a deciding factor in most of those tournaments—including the one Jim Ferrier won in 1951, when he successfully defended his Canadian title.

walked away with Canadian Open titles, Mississaugua has also served up tasty bits of golf history from its home and native land.

Its own story goes back to 1905, a year after the Open was first played. The course got a facelift from legendary designer Stanley Thompson in the 1920s and for 40 years was home to a dapper, stogie-smoking club professional. Even after he retired in 1971, the legendary Gord Brydson played, taught and shot the breeze with his cronies until his death in 2001. Brydson won several Ontario and national titles, and while Pat Fletcher is renowned for being the last Canadian to win the national Open in 1954, Brydson was runner-up. A Canadian Golf Hall of Fame member, Brydson was also the top Canadian pro at the 1942 Open, played right at his home club. "He was a fantastic player," recalled current head professional Gar Hamilton, who has played in eight Canadian Opens himself.

Not only did Mississaugua club pros travel to play in the Open, but the world's greatest players came to take on Mississaugua, and it didn't always turn out well for them. In 1965, the great Jack Nicklaus payed the price on the 12th hole—the "Big Chief," as it's known—by going for its elevated green in two. The wind caught his ball, which rolled down the bank to the river's edge. The Golden Bear took a bogey, lost by one stroke to Gene Littler and never did win the Canadian Open.

In the second round of the 1974 Open, Chi Chi Rodriguez and Larry Ziegler shot 63s to set a course record, but it was a steady Bobby Nichols who prevailed over the entire four rounds.

"Lighthorse" Harry Cooper took a two-stroke penalty when he hit his ball out of bounds on the final hole of the 1938 Open, allowing Sam Snead to tie and force a playoff eventually won by the Slammer. It was the first of three Canadian titles won by Snead.

The Canadian Open was also played at Mississaugua in 1931, 1942 and 1951 and it rightfully takes its place among the great golf courses in this country.

And the reasons for that are both apparent and intangible.

ABOVE A late winter storm and July drought stunted the growth on the fairways and greens at Mississaugua for the 1974 Canadian Open and made the course vulnerable to the professionals. Larry Ziegler (above) and Chi Chi Rodriguez both shot course-record 63s but were unable to capitalize, finishing second and fourth, respectively, behind winner Bobby Nichols.

OPPOSITE The final round of the 1965 Canadian Open was set for a duel between Jack Nicklaus and Arnold Palmer. Palmer took himself out of the race early and Nicklaus had the lead heading to the par-five 12th hole, but he came up short when he went for the green in two and took a bogey. Gene Littler, playing in the group behind, laid up and made birdie to go one ahead—a lead he wouldn't relinquish.

Official Programme

CANADIAN OP
1942
ROYAL CANADIAN GOLF ASSOCIATI

PAIRINGS AND STARTING
THURSDAY, AUGUST 6
AND
FRIDAY, AUGUST 7

MISSISSAUGA GOLF AND
TORONTO

MISSISSAUGUA GOLF AND COUNTRY CLUB

Mississauga, Ontario   DESIGNER: George Cumming/Stanley Thompson

1931   FORMAT: 72 holes, 3 days   PURSE: $1,485, 1st place $500
DATE: July 9–11   WINNER: Walter Hagen, *Detroit, Michigan*   282
YARDAGE: 6,545   PAR: 72   RUNNER-UP: Percy Allis, *Germany*   282
FIELD: 154   CUT: 150   After 36-hole playoff: Hagen, 131; Allis, 142

1938   FORMAT: 72 holes, 3 days   PURSE: $3,000, 1st place $1,000
DATE: August 18–20   WINNER: Sam Snead, *White Sulphur Springs, West Virginia*   277
YARDAGE: 6,545   PAR: 72   RUNNER-UP: Harry Cooper, *Chicopee, Massachusetts*   277
FIELD: 167   CUT: Low 60 and ties   Playoff: 27-hole medal play won by Snead

1942   FORMAT: 72 holes, 3 days   PURSE: $3,000, 1st place $1,000
DATE: August 6–8   WINNER: Craig Wood, *Mamaroneck, New York*   275
YARDAGE: 6,543   PAR: 72   RUNNER-UP: Mike Turnesa, *White Plains, New York*   279
FIELD: 115   CUT: low 60 and ties

1951   FORMAT: 72 holes, 4 days   PURSE: $15,000, 1st place $2,250
DATE: July 5–7   WINNER: Jim Ferrier, *San Francisco, California*   273
YARDAGE: 6,543   PAR: 72   RUNNERS-UP: Fred Hawkins, *El Paso, Texas*   275
FIELD: 134   CUT: 63 players at 152   Ed Oliver, *Seattle, Washington*   275

1965   FORMAT: 72 holes, 4 days   PURSE: $100,000, 1st place $20,000
DATE: July 14–17   WINNER: Gene Littler, *Las Vegas, Nevada*   273
YARDAGE: 6,828   PAR: 70   RUNNER-UP: Jack Nicklaus, *Columbus, Ohio*   274
FIELD: 144   CUT: 73 players

1974   FORMAT: 72 holes, 4 days   PURSE: $200,000, 1st place $40,000
DATE: July 25–28   WINNER: Bobby Nichols, *Akron, Ohio*   270
YARDAGE: 6,788   PAR: 70   RUNNERS-UP: John Schlee, *Carollton, Texas*   274
FIELD: 151   CUT: 73 players at 141   Larry Ziegler, *Terre du Lac, Missouri*   274

1965 CANADIAN OPEN
SATURDAY
ADMISSION $5.00
Nº 10062

FAR LEFT Head professional at Mississaugua from 1932 to 1971, Gordie Brydson was one of the most accomplished Canadian golf pros of his era and an exceptional all-around athlete who played professional hockey for the Toronto Maple Leafs and football for the Toronto Argonauts. Brydson won two CPGA titles and was the low Canadian at the Open on two occasions, including 1942, when the tournament was played over his home course. He also finished runner-up to Pat Fletcher in 1954.

British Columbia

by BRAD ZIEMER

As the Canadian Open celebrates its centennial, golf fans in British Columbia eagerly anticipate the 101st anniversary of our national championship. In 2005, the Bell Canadian Open at long last returns to Vancouver. It will mark just the fourth occasion the tournament has been held on the west coast, and for the third time it will be contested at a course called Shaughnessy.

Thinking it would help sell the city's first residential subdivision, the Canadian Pacific Railway built Shaughnessy Heights, or Old Shaughnessy, as the oldtimers like to call it. One of the first golf courses built within the city limits of Vancouver, it opened for play in 1912, and 36 years later, back in 1948, it played host to the inaugural west coast Open. C.W. (Chuck) Congdon, of Tacoma, Washington, held off a field that included Cary Middlecoff and Lloyd Mangrum to win. Congdon's share of the $9,000 purse was $2,000.

In 1966, the Canadian Open returned to Shaughnessy, or rather New Shaughnessy. The 50-year lease at Shaughnessy Heights expired in the late 1950s and the course is now home to upscale houses and

ABOVE Stan Leonard, of Vancouver's Marine Drive Golf Club, never won the Canadian Open, but he did finish as the low Canadian a record nine times. His best finish was a tie for third in 1946.

OPPOSITE The Canadian Open travelled west of Ontario for the first time in 1948, landing at Shaughnessy Heights Golf Club in Vancouver, where Charles Congdon sealed his victory on the 16th hole with a 150-yard bunker shot that stopped eight feet from the cup. The birdie gave him the lead and Congdon went on to win by three shots.

the Van Dusen Botanical Gardens. Shaughnessy's membership constructed a new course, the Shaughnessy Golf and Country Club, on Musqueam First Nation reserve land on Vancouver's Southwest Marine Drive. The tree-lined course, designed by noted architect A.V. Macan, opened for play in 1960. Six years later, the Open was held during a wet, early fall week.

The weather, and Shaughnessy's tough setup, took its toll on the field. Dave Hill called the course too tough and went home after one practice round. Jack Nicklaus, Billy Casper and Al Geiberger had won the three major U.S.-based championships earlier that year, but none was a factor at Shaughnessy. Texan Don Massengale pitched in for eagle on the 16th hole during the final round en route to a three-shot win over gallery favourite Chi Chi Rodriguez.

The two Canadian Opens contested at the two Shaughnessys served as bookends to the 1954 championship held at Point Grey Golf and Country Club, which has become Vancouver's best-known Canadian Open, thanks in no small part to a club pro named Pat Fletcher. Fifty years ago, Fletcher became the last Canadian to win the Canadian Open—a fact Canadian pros are annually reminded of in the days leading up to the tournament.

Fletcher's victory, which has become more significant as the years have passed, came on a busy weekend for sports in Vancouver. The same weekend Fletcher was presented with the $3,000 winner's cheque, across town at Empire Stadium, during the British Empire Games, Roger Bannister was beating John Landy in what became known as the Miracle Mile.

By the time the 2005 Open drops anchor at Shaughnessy, it will have been 39 years since the tournament was last contested in Vancouver. And if you're looking to place a friendly wager on the winning score, 280 might not be a bad bet. That's exactly how many strokes Congdon, Fletcher and Massengale each recorded to win their west coast Canadian Opens.

LEFT Pat Fletcher made history in 1954. The professional from Saskatoon broke a 40-year dry spell for Canadians when he won the Open at Point Grey Golf and Country Club.

FOLLOWING PAGE By the time the Open returned to British Columbia in 1966, the Shaughnessy Heights club had relocated and was now known simply as the Shaughnessy Golf and Country Club. Texan Don Massengale edged Chi Chi Rodriguez by two shots to win the title.

SHAUGHNESSY HEIGHTS GOLF CLUB

Vancouver, British Columbia YARDAGE: 6,600   PAR: 72   DESIGNER: A.V. Macan

1948 FORMAT: 72 holes, 4 days   PURSE: $9,000, 1st place $2,000
    DATE: September 22–25   WINNER: Chuck Congdon, *Tacoma, Washington*   280
    FIELD: 135   CUT: 60 players at 146   RUNNERS-UP: Dick Metz, *Virginia Beach, Virginia*   283
                             Vic Ghezzi, *Englewood, NY*   283

POINT GREY GOLF AND COUNTRY CLUB

Vancouver, British Columbia YARDAGE: 6,400   PAR: 71   DESIGNER: Geoffrey S. Cornish

1954 FORMAT: 72 holes, 4 days   PURSE: $15,000, 1st place $3,000
    DATE: July 14–17   WINNER: Pat Fletcher, *Saskatoon, Saskatchewan*   280
    FIELD: 135   CUT: 60 players at 158   RUNNERS-UP: Gordon Brydson, *Mississauga, Ontario*   284
                             Bill Welch, *Kennewick, Washington*   284

SHAUGHNESSY GOLF AND COUNTRY CLUB

Vancouver, British Columbia YARDAGE: 6,907   PAR: 71   DESIGNER: A.V. Macan

1966 FORMAT: 72 holes, 4 days   PURSE: $100,000, 1st place $20,000
    DATE: September 29–October 2   WINNER: Don Massengale, *Jacksboro, Texas*   280
    FIELD: N/A   CUT: 74 players at 151   RUNNER-UP: Chi Chi Rodriguez, *Dorado Beach, Puerto Rico*   283

Royal York / St. George's Golf & Country Club

by JAMES BARCLAY

T he Royal York Golf Club—it became St. George's Golf and Country Club in 1946—was host to the Canadian Open in 1933, 1949, 1960 and 1968 on a course designed by Canada's Stanley Thompson.

In 1933, the RCGA had not yet sought a sponsor; the prize money was a mere $1,465 and the four leading players on the PGA Tour didn't show up. But there was still an outstanding field that included Gene Sarazen (who had won the PGA Championship the previous week) Leo Diegel (already a four-time winner of our Open) and the 1932 winner, "Lighthorse" Harry Cooper.

Canadians were reasonably confident that a Canadian could win, hopes that were bolstered when Rex Alston, the pro at Ottawa's Rivermead club, led the field at the halfway mark.

Alas, it was not to be. Some 3,000 to 5,000 spectators on the final day, Saturday, saw an Australian on the PGA Tour, Joe Kirkwood— who made more money as a trick-shot artist than as a touring

ABOVE Opened in 1929, the Royal York Golf Club was planned to be a weekend spot for clients of the Royal York Hotel. Designed by Canada's Stanley Thompson, it is still considered one of the finest courses in Canada. In 1946, it left behind the connection to the Royal York and was renamed St. George's Golf and Country Club.

OPPOSITE St. George's Golf and Country Club has hosted four Canadian Opens: 1933, 1949, 1960 and 1968. The purse at the first was $1,465, but by 1968 it had increased to a whopping $125,000.

On the ticket:
401
ROYAL CANADIAN GOLF ASSOCIATION
OPEN CHAMPIONSHIP
1933
Entire Tournament
$2.50

ABOVE The 1960 Open saw Canadian Al Balding challenge for the title after a first-round and course-record 64 left him one shot out of the lead. A second-round 77 the next day put any hopes of a Canadian win to rest, however, as Balding finished 15 shots behind the champion, Art Wall Jr.

pro—play the finest two rounds of his life, 70–69, for a winning total of four-under 282.

By 1949, Seagram was sponsoring the Open and the purse had gone up to $9,200. The month was June, and the course had no watering system and was playing much shorter than its 6,645 yards. The long hitters were driving the ball through the fairways, so it isn't surprising to find the winner in a short hitter but accurate ball striker, Ernest Jerome Harrison—usually known as "Dutch." An estimated 5,000 to 10,000 spectators attended on the final day.

The 1960 Open, with prize money now at $25,000, wasn't one of the most exciting, although it had a then-record attendance for an Open (over 35,000) with 10,000 on the last day. In the opening round, Canada's Al Balding shot a new course record of 64, raising fresh hopes. But the winner was the far from exciting, far from glamorous Art Wall Jr., who made the St. George's course look ridiculously easy by shooting 19-under par 288.

Some 145 golfers from 10 countries played in the 1968 Open, seeking a share of the $125,000 purse. History was made that week: For the first time in Toronto, the final round was played on a Sunday; the Open was won by a left-hander; and the final day's gallery, estimated at over 35,000, was a record for a Toronto club. The course had been significantly toughened. It now played to 6,792 yards with a par of 70 and had lusher fairways (they were now watered). And that Open was to be among the most dramatic tournaments ever held at the club. Canada's George Knudson, having his most successful year on the PGA Tour, shot a 64 in round three and was tied for the lead with the left-hander from Australia, Bob Charles. But on the final day, George became George and the excitement centered around Charles and Jack Nicklaus. They came to the 18th tied for the lead. On the advice of his caddy, Charles hit his second shot with a 7-iron inches from the pin, while Nicklaus bogeyed.

ABOVE The 1968 Canadian Open was probably the best chance for George Knudson to win on home soil. He came to St. George's having his best year on the Tour and after a third-round 64 was tied for the 54-hole lead. Knudson's Achilles heel—his putting—proved to be his undoing in the final round, however. He struggled to a 73 and finished tied for 10th.

RIGHT After rounds of 67 and 68, Australian Bruce Devlin held a three-stroke advantage through 36 holes, but his hot putter cooled considerably during the third round, where a 75 left him two strokes behind the leaders. He eventually finished tied for 10th.

OPPOSITE Headed to the final hole of the 1968 tournament, New Zealander Bob Charles was nursing a one-shot lead over Jack Nicklaus. The first to play his approach, Charles calmly hit his 7-iron inches from the cup to secure his victory— the first by a left-handed golfer.

ROYAL YORK/ST. GEORGE'S GOLF & COUNTRY CLUB

Toronto, Ontario   DESIGNER: Stanley Thompson

1933		
FORMAT: 72 holes, 3 days	PURSE: $1,465, 1st place $500	
DATE: August 17–19	WINNER: Joe Kirkwood, *Chicago, Illinois*	282
YARDAGE: 6,575 PAR: 72	RUNNERS-UP: Lex Robson, *Islington, Ontario*	290
FIELD: 141 CUT: low 60 and ties	Harry Cooper, *Chicago, Illinois*	290

1949		
FORMAT: 72 holes, 4 days	PURSE: $9,200, 1st place $2,000	
DATE: June 22–25	WINNER: E. J. "Dutch" Harrison, *Little Rock, Arkansas*	271
YARDAGE: 6,645 PAR: 72	RUNNER-UP: Jim Ferrier, *San Francisco, California*	275
FIELD: 184 CUT: 66 players at 155		

1960		
FORMAT: 72 holes, 4 days	PURSE: $25,000, 1st place $3,500	
DATE: July 6–9	WINNER: Art Wall Jr, *Pocono Manor, Pennsylvania*	269
YARDAGE: 6,710 PAR: 72	RUNNERS-UP: Jay Hebert, *Lafayette, Louisiana*	275
FIELD: 150 CUT: 62 players at 218	Bob Goalby, *Crystal River, Florida*	275

1968		
FORMAT: 72 holes, 4 days	PURSE: $125,000, 1st place $25,000	
DATE: June 20–23	WINNER: Bob Charles, *Christchurch, New Zealand*	274
YARDAGE: 6,792 PAR: 70	RUNNER-UP: Jack Nicklaus, *Columbus, Ohio*	276
FIELD: 150 CUT: 71 players at 147		

The Prairies

by TIM CAMPBELL

Nearing the 50th anniversary of the first championship, the Canadian Open went down a new road in 1952 with its first of three Prairie Opens in a nine-year stretch.

The first of these was conducted at Winnipeg's St. Charles Country Club, one of Manitoba's oldest clubs. Six years later, in 1958, the RCGA was again in the west for the national Open, this time at Edmonton's stately Mayfair Golf and Country Club. And the third and final mid-country Open to date was held at Winnipeg's Niakwa Country Club in 1961.

The 1952 Open will not only be remembered as the first championship away from the big centres of east or west, but also as the one featuring a scoring record that still stands as modern-era players head for the 2004 championship at Glen Abbey. Johnny Palmer, of North Carolina, by all reports a mild-mannered, unobtrusive type, assaulted the record books like never before. Palmer's 72-hole total of 263 is unmatched to this day.

ABOVE AND OPPOSITE In 1958, Edmonton's Mayfair Golf and Country Club hosted Alberta's only Canadian Open. Twenty-six year-old Wes Ellis was nine-under-par over the final two rounds and edged Jay Herbert by a single stroke. With three holes to play, Ellis seemed secure with a three-shot lead, but after bogeying the 17th hole, and landing his approach at the final hole in a greenside bunker, a playoff loomed. But Ellis got up-and-down, and his total of 267 was good enough for the win.

ABOVE Winnipeg's St. Charles Country Club hosted the 1952 Canadian Open and saw Johnny Palmer set the 72-hole scoring record of 263 that still stands after more than 50 years. Palmer's rounds of 66–65–66–66 bettered the old mark, set by Bobby Locke in 1947, by five shots.

OPPOSITE Charlie Sifford putts over the rain-soaked Niakwa Country Club in Winnipeg at the 1961 "umbrella" Open. The winner, Jacky Cupit, was only one year into his professional career when he won the title by five strokes over a group of players that included his older brother, Buster.

Mother Nature also had a hand in the scoring record. St. Charles' 6,377-yard layout for the championship had been doused with generous rains during the summer, but when tournament week arrived, there was nothing but good weather and next to no wind. On the perfectly conditioned greens in Winnipeg, Palmer never had more than 29 putts on a given day and the engravers were etching his name into the Seagram Gold Cup long before showers arrived for the final 90 minutes of the fourth round.

There was no such runaway when the Tour gathered in mid-August at Mayfair in Edmonton for the 1958 Open. The leader board was tightly packed each day, and unheralded Texan Wes Ellis Jr. stormed out of the field on the final nine holes to grab the championship by a single shot over Jay Hebert.

Perfect weather and course conditions, as in Winnipeg six years earlier, led to a scoring bonanza on the par-70, 6,657-yard course. Through three rounds, Hebert had taken command at 11-under, two better than Ellis, Bob Goetz and Tom Jacobs. Ellis, however, went out in two-under 33 in the final round and drew clear of the field with three straight birdies on the back nine. In the lead, Ellis three-putted the par-three 71st hole, missing from 18 inches, and then bunkered his approach to the final green of regulation play. He blasted out to 12 feet above the hole but ran in the par putt for a round of 66, a 13-under total of 267 and the one-shot win over Hebert.

When the Canadian Open moved back to Winnipeg for the 1961 championship, the elements reversed themselves from Palmer's scoring exploits nine years before. Niakwa's Open will always be known as the "umbrella" Open. A perfect and dry summer was underway in Manitoba, leading to immaculate course conditions at the old Stanley Thompson layout of 6,426 yards. But just minutes before Wednesday's first round began, the rain began and the downpour continued through four rounds, finally halting only when Jacky Cupit came forward to receive the champion's trophy. The entire summer was dry in Winnipeg, save for those four days in July.

Cupit, a 23-year-old from Texas, broke out of a 36-hole tie with Tony Lema by firing a six-under 64 in the third round. Cupit led his older brother, Buster, by a shot, 199–200, heading for the final day, and even though he shot 71 on Saturday, Cupit coasted to an easy five-shot victory over Buster, Dow Finsterwald and Bobby Nichols.

ST. CHARLES COUNTRY CLUB

Winnipeg, Manitoba   YARDAGE: 6,377   PAR: 72   DESIGNER: Donald Ross

1952 FORMAT: 72 holes, 4 days   PURSE: $15,000, 1st place $3,000
         DATE: July 16–19   WINNER: Johnny Palmer, *Badin, North Carolina*   263
         FIELD: 142   CUT: 60 players at 149   RUNNERS-UP: Dick Mayer, *St. Petersburg, Florida*   274
                                          Fred Haas Jr., *New Orleans, Louisiana*   274

MAYFAIR GOLF AND COUNTRY CLUB

Edmonton, Alberta   YARDAGE: 6,657   PAR: 70   DESIGNER: Stanley Thompson

1958 FORMAT: 72 holes, 4 days   PURSE: $25,000, 1st place $3,500
         DATE: August 20–23   WINNER: Wesley Ellis Jr., *Ridgewood, New Jersey*   267
         FIELD: 106   CUT: 41 players at 142   RUNNER-UP: Jay Hebert, *Sanford, Florida*   268

NIAKWA COUNTRY CLUB

Winnipeg, Manitoba   YARDAGE: 6,426   PAR: 70   DESIGNER: Stanley Thompson

1961 FORMAT: 72 holes, 4 days   PURSE: $30,000, 1st place $4,300
         DATE: July 12–15   WINNER: Jacky Cupit, *Longview, Texas*   270
         FIELD: 145   CUT: 65 players at 150   RUNNERS-UP: Dow Finsterwald, *Tequesta, Florida*   275
                                          Buster Cupit, *Fort Smith, Arizona*   275
                                          Bobby Nichols, *Midland Texas*   275

Southwestern Ontario

by RICK YOUNG

Fashioning some of the world's most compelling and celebrated golf courses is a testament to the brilliance of architectural giants Donald Ross, Walter J. Travis, Stanley Thompson and Robert Trent Jones Sr. And four of those courses—Essex Golf and Country Club near Windsor, The Cherry Hill Club in Ridgeway, Westmount Golf and Country Club in Kitchener and the London Hunt and Country Club—have been and shall always be some of my personal favourites. If you grew up in southwestern Ontario, these were the courses you heard about, read about; the ones you dreamed of playing. Being granted the privilege of a round on any of the four was like taking home a trophy, something to be admired and envied by your golfing friends. Of course, the traditional aura of these land canvases goes beyond the design artists who rendered them into 18-hole masterpieces. Possessing an admired and envied trophy of their own, each of these distinctly parkland layouts has staged the Canadian Open, further acknowledgement of the status they enjoy as four of this nation's finest.

ABOVE Essex Golf and Country Club, near Windsor, came to the rescue in 1976 when the newly-built Glen Abbey wasn't ready to host the Canadian Open. George Knudson (putting) came to town with high expectations after capturing the Canadian PGA Championship, but he missed the cut.

OPPOSITE Canadian Al Balding at the 1957 Open. Westmount didn't look promising after the first round, when players blasted the course conditions and setup. But their tune changed as the week went by, and when Bayer was presented with the Seagram Gold Cup, he had nothing but praise for Westmount.

ABOVE The Westmount Golf and Country Club hosted the 1957 Canadian Open, where big George Bayer (left) captured the title by two strokes. With Bayer are PGA champion Jim Turnesa (centre) and U.S. Open winner Julius Boros.

As the Canadian Open celebrates 100 years, the western Ontario chapter begins in Kitchener.

Staking its humble beginnings on the purchase of land on the outskirts of the Oktoberfest city in 1929, Westmount welcomed the world's best players, including long-hitting George Bayer, the eventual champion in 1957. Though fairway height and collars around the greens sparked widespread debate during the week, there was no disputing the Stanley Thompson-designed attributes of Westmount as a venue. "I don't know what the fuss is about," suggested former Masters champion Doug Ford. "This is one of the finest courses I've ever played."

In 1970, the RCGA brought the Canadian Open to London, Ontario, and its hallowed Hunt and Country Club. The atmosphere in the golf-crazed Forest City was electric. Designed by Robert Trent Jones in 1960, the course proved a stern test, even for champion Kermit Zarley of Texas, who staved off fellow American Gibby Gilbert to win with an aggregate of 279. "As we expected," said Sandy Somerville, the 1932 United States Amateur champion and a longtime Hunt Club member, "the golf course tested every facet of the players' games."

The Open returned to southwestern Ontario in 1972, this time to the Travis-inspired Cherry Hill in the tiny Niagara town of

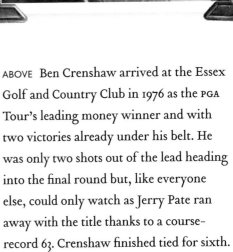

ABOVE Ben Crenshaw arrived at the Essex Golf and Country Club in 1976 as the PGA Tour's leading money winner and with two victories already under his belt. He was only two shots out of the lead heading into the final round but, like everyone else, could only watch as Jerry Pate ran away with the title thanks to a course-record 63. Crenshaw finished tied for sixth.

LEFT The 1957 Open at the Westmount Golf and Country Club.

Ridgeway. It was a popular choice of venue. Founded by six prominent Buffalo, New York businessmen, Cherry Hill drew rave reviews. "It's by far the finest test of golf I've ever played in Canada," said champion Gay Brewer. Added former Canadian Open champion Arnold Palmer, "Next year's Open should be right back here at Cherry Hill."

A three-time Canadian Open bridesmaid, Jack Nicklaus descended on the Windsor suburb of Lasalle in 1976 to stately Essex, a golf course crafted by his favourite designer—Donald Ross. After three rounds, Nicklaus seemed poised to capture professional golf's coveted "fifth major." But the reigning U.S. Open champion had

WESTMOUNT GOLF AND COUNTRY CLUB

Kitchener, Ontario   YARDAGE: 6,444   PAR: 71   DESIGNER: Stanley Thompson

1957 FORMAT: 72 holes, 4 days   PURSE: $25,000, 1st place $3,500
        DATE: July 10–13   WINNER: George Bayer, *San Gabriel, California*   271
        FIELD: 191   CUT: 103 players at 151   RUNNER-UP: Bo Wininger, *Odessa, Texas*   273

LONDON HUNT AND COUNTRY CLUB

London, Ontario   YARDAGE: 7,168   PAR: 72   DESIGNER: Robert Trent Jones

1970 FORMAT: 72 holes, 4 days   PURSE: $125,000, 1st place $25,000
        DATE: July 2–5   WINNER: Kermit Zarley, *Houston, Texas*   279
        FIELD: 144   CUT: 71 players at 147   RUNNER-UP: Gibby Gilbert, *Hollywood, Florida*   282

THE CHERRY HILL CLUB, LTD.

Ridgeway, Ontario   YARDAGE: 6,751   PAR: 71   DESIGNER: Walter J. Travis

1972 FORMAT: 72 holes, 4 days   PURSE: $150,000, 1st place $30,000
        DATE: July 6–9   WINNER: Gay Brewer Jr., *Dallas, Texas*   275
        FIELD: 150   CUT: 73 players at 147   RUNNERS-UP: Sam Adams, *Boone, North Carolina*   276
        Dave Hill, *Jackson, Missouri*   276

ESSEX GOLF AND COUNTRY CLUB

Windsor, Ontario   YARDAGE: 6,696   PAR: 70   DESIGNER: Donald Ross

1976 FORMAT: 72 holes, 4 days   PURSE: $200,000, 1st place $40,000
        DATE: July 22–25   WINNER: Jerry Pate, *Pensacola, Florida*   267
        FIELD: 149   CUT: 79 players at 144   RUNNER-UP: Jack Nicklaus, *Muirfield Village, Ohio*   271

RIGHT In 1972 Rod McIsaac of Great Northern Capital (later Genstar), found out first-hand the difficulties courses like Cherry Hill posed for spectators. After the tournament he approached RCGA officials with the idea of turning his company's Oakville golf course into a permanent location for the Canadian Open.

other ideas. Jerry Pate blistered Essex with a course-record 63 on the final day to take the title and break the hearts of Nicklaus fans coast to coast. In the gallery that fateful Sunday, my heart was one of them. "Coming from behind and defeating Jack was a big moment," said Pate. "I was so comfortable with my game that day. And being a Ross design, I was pretty excited. It was an outstanding golf course"—just as Essex, Westmount, Cherry Hill and the Hunt Club were back then and still are today.

Glen Abbey Golf Club

by LORNE RUBENSTEIN

The Royal Canadian Golf Association and the Glen Abbey Golf Club have played important roles in my golf-writing life. I worked for the RCGA's museum, Hall of Fame and library when it moved its headquarters from downtown Toronto to the Abbey in 1975. I walked the course one gloomy June day when Jack Nicklaus and Tom Weiskopf opened the course with an exhibition round—Weiskopf hit the most elegant 3-wood within a few feet of the last hole and made his eagle—and I attended almost every Canadian Open there between 1977 and 2000.

Many highlights come to mind. I'll focus on only a few.

Richard Zokol was tied for the lead with Curtis Strange after three rounds of the 1987 Canadian Open but got off to a weak start, eventually shot 75 and fell back to seventh place. I remember the dignity with which Zokol carried himself that difficult day, when Canadians hoped he would bring the championship here again.

The same year I followed Jim Nelford as he finished 18th. Nelford had been seriously injured in a waterskiing accident in September 1985.

ABOVE Glen Abbey ultimately changed the face not only of the Open but also of Canadian golf itself. The Jack Nicklaus-designed course was to host 23 of the next 25 Opens beginning in 1977. Four years later, Genstar sold the property to the RCGA for $3 million. In 1998, with golf's popularity on the rise and the Open one of the premier sporting events in the country, ClubLink purchased Glen Abbey at more than 10 times the fee the RCGA struggled to pay in the 1980s.

OPPOSITE Over the years, many an Open has been won or lost on Glen Abbey's par-five 18th hole, making the walk down the fairway short for some and longer for others.

ABOVE A fundamental part of the growth of the tournament into today's Bell Canadian Open was the move to Glen Abbey. In 1974 the RCGA signed an agreement to reconstruct an Oakville golf course into a spectator-friendly permanent home for the Open. Pictured left to right are RCGA Executive Director Bruce Forbes, clubhouse architect Brian Bancroft and 1974 RCGA President Richard Grimm.

OPPOSITE The second Open at Glen Abbey proved the course was of championship calibre. Winner Bruce Lietzke was the only player to break par, but even he had to admit that he hadn't played his best and simply "survived it better than anyone else."

It looked for a while like he might never hit a ball again, let alone compete on the PGA Tour. But he came back and played gallantly with only half the strength in his right arm. I can still hear the cheers from the thousands of spectators massed around the final green in front of the Abbey's clubhouse.

Seven years later, in 1994, Nick Price curved a glorious 2-iron from 217 yards, around a tree from the left side of the 16th fairway to within a couple of feet of the hole. The eagle gave him a two-shot lead and he went on to win the tournament. The next year, I spoke during the dinner when Jack Nicklaus was inducted into the Canadian Golf Hall of Fame. Nicklaus was so proud of Glen Abbey, the first course he designed all on his own. After dinner, my wife Nell and I walked Nicklaus and his wife Barbara back to their car. Nicklaus stopped, looked out over the course in the moonlight and mentioned how glad he was of the opportunity the RCGA had given him at Glen Abbey. He embarked from there on a journey of designing courses around the world that continues today.

The Abbey also continues. From a pub in Dornoch, high up in the Scottish Highlands, I watched Tiger Woods hit that towering 6-iron from a bunker and over the water to win the 2000 Bell Canadian Open. I was with a few Canadian friends, and we all felt connected to the Abbey. The RCGA doesn't own the course anymore, but I still think of it as theirs. It's often said that home is where the heart is. For me, Glen Abbey will always feel like the home of Canadian golf.

Canadian Open 78
Glen Abbey GOLF CLUB
JUNE 19-25
Oakville, Ontario
Conducted by
The Royal Canadian Golf
Association
Presented by
Peter Jackson
NO CAMERAS
TICKET

GLEN ABBEY GOLF CLUB

Oakville, Ontario   DESIGNER: Jack Nicklaus

1977 FORMAT: 72 holes, 4 days   PURSE: $225,000, 1st place $45,000
DATE: July 21–24   WINNER: Lee Trevino, *St. Teresa, New Mexico*   280
YARDAGE: 7,096   PAR: 72   RUNNER-UP: Peter Oosterhuis, *Palm Springs, California*   284
FIELD: 156   CUT: 72 players at 150

1978 FORMAT: 72 holes, 4 days   PURSE: $250,000, 1st place $50,000
DATE: June 22–25   WINNER: Bruce Lietzke, *Beaumont, Texas*   283
YARDAGE: 7,050   PAR: 71   RUNNER-UP: Pat McGowan, *Colusa, California*   284
FIELD: 157   CUT: 71 players at 151

1979 FORMAT: 72 holes, 4 days   PURSE: $350,000, 1st place $63,000
DATE: June 21–24   WINNER: Lee Trevino, *Dallas, Texas*   281
YARDAGE: 7,059   PAR: 71   RUNNER-UP: Ben Crenshaw, *Austin, Texas*   284
FIELD: 156   CUT: 71 players at 148

continued...

1981
FORMAT: 72 holes, 4 days
DATE: July 30–August 2
YARDAGE: 7,060 PAR: 71
FIELD: 140   CUT: 73 players at 148

PURSE: $425,000, 1st place $76,500
WINNER: Peter Oosterhuis, *Santa Barbara, California* 280
RUNNERS-UP: Bruce Lietzke, *Jay, Oklahoma* 281
    Jack Nicklaus, *Muirfield Village, Ohio* 281
    Andy North, *Madison, Wisconsin* 281

1982
FORMAT: 72 holes, 4 days
DATE: July 29–August 1
YARDAGE: 7,060 PAR: 71
FIELD: 150   CUT: 74 players at 145

PURSE: $425,000, 1st place $76,500
WINNER: Bruce Lietzke, *Afton, Oklahoma* 277
RUNNER-UP: Hal Sutton, *Shreveport, Louisiana* 279

1983
FORMAT: 72 holes, 4 days
DATE: July 28–31
YARDAGE: 7,055 PAR: 71
FIELD: 143   CUT: 80 players at 147

PURSE: $425,000, 1st place $63,000
WINNER: John Cook, *Rancho Mirage, California* 277
RUNNER-UP: Johnny Miller, *Mapleton, Utah* 277
Playoff: Sudden-death, to six extra holes

1984
FORMAT: 72 holes, 4 days
DATE: June 28–July 1
YARDAGE: 7,102 PAR: 72
FIELD: 153   CUT: 77 players at 150

PURSE: $525,000, 1st place $72,000
WINNER: Greg Norman, *Orlando, Florida* 278
RUNNER-UP: Jack Nicklaus, *Muirfield Village, Ohio* 280

1985
FORMAT: 72 holes, 4 days
DATE: July 4–7
YARDAGE: 7,102 PAR: 72
FIELD: 148   CUT: 72 players at 148

PURSE: $750,000, 1st place $86,506.52
WINNER: Curtis Strange, *Kingsmill, Virginia* 279
RUNNERS-UP: Jack Nicklaus, *Muirfield Village, Ohio* 281
    Greg Norman, *Orlando, Florida* 281

1986
FORMAT: 72 holes, 4 days
DATE: June 26–29
YARDAGE: 7,102 PAR: 72
FIELD: 152   CUT: 75 players at 148

PURSE: $850,000, 1st place $108,000
WINNER: Bob Murphy, *Stuart, Florida* 280
RUNNER-UP: Greg Norman, *Orlando, Florida* 283

1987
FORMAT: 72 holes, 4 days
DATE: July 2–5
YARDAGE: 7,102 PAR: 72
FIELD: 157   CUT: 71 players at 147

PURSE: $850,000, 1st place $108,000
WINNER: Curtis Strange, *Kingsmill, Virginia* 276
RUNNERS-UP: David Frost, *Dallas, Texas* 279
    Jodie Mudd, *Louisville, Kentucky* 279
    Nick Price, *Orlando, Florida* 279

1988
FORMAT: 72 holes, 4 days
DATE: September 1–4
YARDAGE: 7,102 PAR: 72
FIELD: 157   CUT: 71 players at 145

PURSE: $900,000, 1st place $135,000
WINNER: Ken Green, *Danbury, Connecticut* 275
RUNNERS-UP: Bill Glasson, *San Diego, California* 276
    Scott Verplank, *Edmond, Oklahoma* 276

1989
FORMAT: 72 holes, 4 days
DATE: June 22–25
YARDAGE: 6,788 PAR: 70
FIELD: 156   CUT: 83 players at 142

PURSE: $1 million, 1st place $162,000
WINNER: Steve Jones, *Phoenix, Arizona* 271
RUNNERS-UP: Clark Burroughs, *Ponte Vedra Beach, Florida* 273
    Mark Calcavecchia, *North Palm Beach Florida* 273
    Mike Hulbert, *Orlando, Florida* 273

1990	FORMAT: 72 holes, 4 days	PURSE: $1 million, 1st place $180,000	
	DATE: September 13–16	WINNER: Wayne Levi, *New Hartford, New York*	278
	YARDAGE: 7,102 PAR: 72	RUNNERS-UP: Ian Baker-Finch, *Queensland, Australia*	279
	FIELD: 156 CUT: 70 players at 145	Jim Woodward, *Oklahoma City, Oklahoma*	279
1991	FORMAT: 72 holes, 4 days	PURSE: $1 million, 1st place $180,000	
	DATE: September 5–8	WINNER: Nick Price, *Lake Mona, Florida*	273
	YARDAGE: 7,102 PAR: 72	RUNNER-UP: David Edwards, *Edmond, Oklahoma*	274
	FIELD: 156 CUT: 80 players at 144		
1992	FORMAT: 72 holes, 4 days	PURSE: $1 million, 1st place $180,000	
	DATE: September 10–13	WINNER: Greg Norman, *Orlando, Florida*	280
	YARDAGE: 7,112 PAR: 72	RUNNER-UP: Bruce Lietzke, *Dallas, Texas*	280
	FIELD: 156 CUT: 72 players at 148	Playoff: Sudden-death, to two extra holes	
1993	FORMAT: 72 holes, 4 days	PURSE: $1 million, 1st place $180,000	
	DATE: September 9–12	WINNER: David Frost, *Dallas, Texas*	279
	YARDAGE: 7,112 PAR: 72	RUNNER-UP: Fred Couples, *South Andros, Bahamas*	280
	FIELD: 156 CUT: 75 players at 148		
1994	FORMAT: 72 holes, 4 days	PURSE: $1.3 million, 1st place $234,000	
	DATE: September 8–11	WINNER: Nick Price, *Lake Nona, Florida*	275
	YARDAGE: 7,112 PAR: 72	RUNNER-UP: Mark Calcavecchia, *West Palm Beach, Florida*	276
	FIELD: 156 CUT: 78 players at 145		
1995	FORMAT: 72 holes, 4 days	PURSE: $1.3 million, 1st place $234,000	
	DATE: September 7–10	WINNER: Mark O'Meara, *Windermere, Florida*	274
	YARDAGE: 7,112 PAR: 72	RUNNER-UP: Bob Lohr, *Orlando, Florida*	274
	FIELD: 156 CUT: 81 players at 147	Playoff: Sudden-death, to one extra hole	
1996	FORMAT: 72 holes, 4 days	PURSE: $1.5 million, 1st place $270,000	
	DATE: September 5–8	WINNER: Dudley Hart, *Fort Lauderdale, Florida*	202
	YARDAGE: 7,112 PAR: 72	RUNNER-UP: David Duval, *Ponte Vedra Beach, Florida*	203
	FIELD: 156 CUT: 77 players at 144	Event shortened to 54 holes due to weather	
1998	FORMAT: 72 holes, 4 days	PURSE: $2.2 million, 1st place $396,000	
	DATE: September 10–13	WINNER: Billy Andrade, *Bristol, Rhode Island*	275
	YARDAGE: 7,112 PAR: 72	RUNNER-UP: Bob Friend, *Pittsburgh, Pennsylvania*	275
	FIELD: 156 CUT: 75 players at 146	Playoff: Sudden-death, to one extra hole	
1999	FORMAT: 72 holes, 4 days	PURSE: $2.5 million, 1st place $450,000	
	DATE: September 9–12	WINNER: Hal Sutton, *Shreveport, Louisiana*	275
	YARDAGE: 7,112 PAR: 72	RUNNER-UP: Dennis Paulson, *Vista, California*	278
	FIELD: 156 CUT: 77 players at 146		
2000	FORMAT: 72 holes, 4 days	PURSE: $3.3 million, 1st place $594,000	
	DATE: September 6–10	WINNER: Tiger Woods, *Windermere, Florida*	266
	YARDAGE: 7,112 PAR: 72	RUNNER-UP: Grant Waite, *Palmerston North, New Zealand*	267
	FIELD: 156 CUT: 73 at 144		

LEFT At the 1979 Canadian Open, Trevino did not play conservatively—he blasted the ball down the monstrous fairways on his way to capturing his third title, joining Leo Diegel (1924, 1925, 1928, 1929), Tommy Armour (1927, 1930, 1934) and Sam Snead (1938, 1940, 1941) as the only players to win the Canadian Open more than twice.

ABOVE LEFT When England's Peter Oosterhuis (left) arrived at Glen Abbey in July of 1981, he was still looking for his first PGA Tour victory. Runner-up to Trevino in 1977, Oosterhuis began the final round three shots behind leader Leonard Thompson, who had posted a course-record 62 in the second round on Friday. Oosterhuis finished with a two-under 70 for a total of 280 and then had to wait. Jack Nicklaus recorded his fifth runner-up finish and had a chance to force a playoff on 18, but his 20-foot eagle putt came up eight inches short.

ABOVE RIGHT In 1982, Bruce Lietzke (right) won his second Canadian Open with a solid final round, maintaining his two-shot lead throughout the day and finishing with a Glen Abbey record of seven-under 277. Playing in his first Open, 1980 U.S. Amateur champion Hal Sutton finished second, a result he'd improve upon 17 years later by winning the title.

The 452-yard 11th at Glen Abbey is widely considered its signature hole. John Daly certainly left his mark there. In fact, a plaque recounting Daly's attempt to reach the green with his tee shot is permanently displayed on the back tee deck. His ball landed in the creek, but Daly still managed a respectable 12th-place finish in his first Canadian Open.

ABOVE The six-hole sudden-death playoff for the 1983 Canadian Open
almost didn't happen—not because either player made a mistake on the
course, but because Johnny Miller shouldn't have been there in the first
place. After gallbladder surgery the previous month, he disobeyed the
wishes of his doctor and arrived at the tournament not having touched a
golf club since before his operation. In the playoff, Miller scrambled to
match John Cook through five playoff holes. Cook, the eventual winner,
was never farther away than 15 feet for birdie, while Miller was forced
to save pars with chips or long lag putts.

ABOVE AND LEFT Nick Price (left) was poised for a wire-to-wire win at the 1984 Canadian Open after a pair of 67s that helped build a six-stroke lead. Even after a one-over 73 on Saturday, he still held a four-stroke lead to start the final round. Paired with Jack Nicklaus (above) and Greg Norman in the final group, Price came undone, shooting a 76 to finish third. Norman out-duelled Nicklaus to win his first of two Canadian Open titles.

FOLLOWING PAGES The 12th hole at Glen Abbey is one of the toughest par threes on the course. Players hit from an elevated tee—used just for the championship— to a green fronted by Sixteen Mile Creek, as well as a few strategically placed bunkers. Dave Barr's fourth-place finish in the 1988 Open was assisted by a hole-in-one at No. 12.

ABOVE Canadian Richard Zokol found himself carrying the hopes of a nation as he entered the final round of the 1987 Open tied for the lead after rounds of 70–68–69. But those hopes would be dashed yet again. Zokol began with a bogey and couldn't buy a birdie putt, shooting a 75 and finishing in a tie for seventh. Said Zokol, "I didn't play well because I didn't put myself in position to make birdies. You can't play solid golf and do that."

LEFT Rookie Davis Love III teed it up at the 1986 Canadian Open and tied for third but got lost in the crowd. All eyes were on the Golden Bear, looking to capture the title after winning his sixth Masters title earlier in the year at the age of 46. The eventual champion, however, was another veteran, 43-year-old Bob Murphy, who edged Greg Norman by three shots for his first PGA Tour victory in 11 years.

RIGHT Curtis Strange won both of his Canadian Open titles at the Abbey. In 1985, he tamed both a bear and a shark, earning a two-stroke victory over Jack Nicklaus and Greg Norman. In 1987, he established a new scoring record for Glen Abbey with 12-under 276— a mark that would stand only a year. It was bettered by Ken Green by a stroke at the next Open.

LEFT The 1988 Open became a five-day affair after rains forced the suspension of play during the final round with 22 players still to finish. Dave Barr (pictured) got his round in and hoped his 11-under might be good enough for a win. It wasn't, but his tie for fourth was his best Open result in more than 25 tries and remains the best finish by a Canadian at Glen Abbey. "If you had said I'd be 11-under at the end of the week, I'd have said it would win the tournament because Glen Abbey is one of the toughest courses we play," Barr said afterwards. Ken Green still had six holes to play when he woke up Monday morning and he made the most of them, finishing at 13-under 275, one shot ahead of Scott Verplank and Bill Glasson.

LEFT Wayne Levi arrived at Glen Abbey in 1990 having already won three times that year on the PGA Tour. Hanging around the leaders all week, Levi's two-under 70 on Sunday was enough to earn him his fourth win of the year, by one stroke over Ian Baker-Finch and Jim Woodward.

OPPOSITE At the 1989 Open, Mark Calcavecchia holed a 7-iron from 160 yards for an ace at the par-three third hole, but it wasn't enough. He finished two shots behind winner Steve Jones. Calcavecchia was a bridesmaid again in 1994.

LEFT Glen Abbey's par-four 17th hole is most remarkable for its unusual green. Wildly shaped, depending on the pin placement, players can feel like they are at the local mini-putt trying to reach the hole. When a bridge was built on nearby Upper Middle Road, the green was altered, but its uniqueness remained. In 1991, it looked as if Ken Green had his second title until he reached 17, where he missed a three-foot par putt and lost his chance to catch eventual champion Nick Price.

ABOVE A despondent Greg Norman came to the Open in 1992 without a tournament win in more than two years. Norman lost a three-shot lead over the last five holes but sank a 12-foot birdie putt to force a playoff with two-time winner Bruce Lietzke. On the second hole of the playoff, Norman hit a 3-wood into the back bunker on 18 and got up-and-down for a birdie to win his second Canadian Open and match Steve Jones's record of the longest span between victories.

The 1993 Open could have been a Cinderella story—but then David Frost crashed the ball. Canadian Tour player Steve Stricker sought to capture the Canadian double, having won that year's CPGA Championship, but sitting one back of the leader on Sunday, he bogeyed four of the first seven holes. Journeyman Brad Bryant, winless on the Tour in 16 years, held a three-shot lead with seven holes to play but bogeyed three of the next four holes. Although 1992 Masters champion Fred Couples (pictured here) birdied all three of the par fives on the back nine, it wasn't enough as South Africa's Frost birdied 16 and 18 to edge Couples by a single stroke.

ABOVE AND RIGHT Nick Price was destined to win the 1994 Open. He was that good, and he was that lucky, too. Twice the recipient of fortuitous bounces at the 11th hole, he hit what he now calls the greatest shot of his career on No. 16 (opposite) to ensure his victory during the final round. Playing the 11th on Thursday, his second hole of the day, Price found himself in a fairway bunker at the 452-yard par-four, but his poorly struck 8-iron hit a rock in the creek and his ball landed on the green, affording him an easy par instead of something worse. On Saturday, Price got more help at the 11th. This time, his tee shot hit a tree on the left and his ball ended up 50 yards ahead and to the right, leaving Price only a sand wedge to the green. He hit his approach to four feet and made birdie. But it was a 2-iron on the par-five 16th that delivered the victory. With 217 yards left to the green, Price struck "probably the best 2-iron I've ever hit" and it rolled to within two feet of the cup. Price's eagle negated Mark Calcavecchia's eagle on 18 and left Price with a one-stroke victory and his second Canadian Open title in four years.

Nick Price's longtime caddie, Jeff "Squeeky" Medlen (centre), died of leukemia in 1997 after helping him not only to a pair of Canadian Open titles (in 1991 and 1994), but also to three major championships, including the 1994 British Open. In 1991, Price began the final round five shots behind D.A. Weibring. Price won the tournament in the valley, where he birdied all five holes (he had also birdied three of the five in Saturday's third round) and finished with three pars. He then watched as his pursuers—Fred Couples, David Edwards and Ken Green—all came up just short.

RIGHT In 1996, Hurricane Fran blew into town on Saturday—play was suspended twice that day and eventually cancelled, marking the first time the tournament had been shortened to 54 holes—and Dudley Hart (top) left Glen Abbey on Sunday as the Bell Canadian Open champion. Hart overcame a three-shot deficit in the third and final round when he caught second-round leader Scott Dunlap at the eighth hole and never looked back, holding on for a one-shot victory over David Duval and becoming one of six players in Canadian Open history to make the Open his first PGA Tour win.

OPPOSITE 1996 also saw Tiger Woods make his Bell Canadian Open debut. His trip to Glen Abbey on a sponsor's exemption was his second PGA Tour event. Tiger finished tied for 11th and followed that up with two wins and three top 10s in only eight starts, finishing 24th on the money list with $790,594 and earning his Tour card for the following year without having to go to Q-School.

ABOVE AND LEFT It wasn't pretty, but in the end Billy Andrade defeated Bob Friend on the first playoff hole to win the 1998 Bell Canadian Open. Andrade trailed Friend by two shots when play began on Sunday and was one ahead when they reached the par-five 18th. Andrade dumped his second shot into the pond fronting the green and sank a 35-foot par putt to force a playoff after Friend made a birdie. Both players stayed away from the water in the playoff, ending up with awkward lies on thin grass where spectators had been sitting. Friend then played his third shot, which bounced through the green and into the water. Andrade decided to play cautiously and purposely chipped into the bunker. When Friend was unable to chip in for a par five, Andrade got up-and-down for his first victory since 1991.

FOLLOWING PAGES In 2000, Tiger Woods duelled with Grant Waite over the final 18 holes before finally subduing the New Zealander on the 72nd with what is probably the most memorable shot of his illustrious career—so far. Holding a one-shot advantage, Woods found his tee shot in a fairway bunker. After watching Waite put his second shot 30 feet from the hole, Woods decided he had no choice but to go for the green. Woods sent a 6-iron over the flag 216 yards away and then had a chip and a putt for the title-clinching birdie. With the victory, Woods became only the second golfer after Lee Trevino to capture the U.S., British and Canadian Opens in the same year, earning him the Triple Crown Trophy.

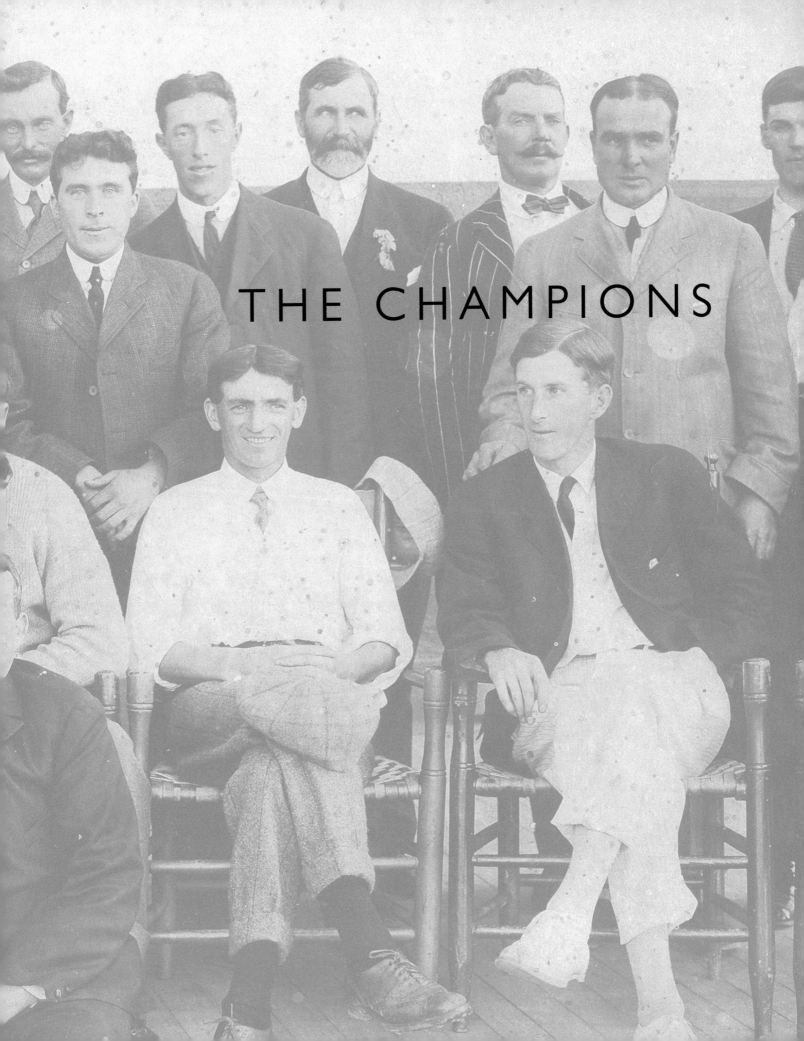

THE CHAMPIONS

The Open Golf Championship of Canada is the third oldest in the world, right behind the British Open (1860) and the U.S. Open (1895), and in the 100 years since it was first played, it has been won by the finest names in golfing history, from Tommy Armour through to Tiger Woods. Those winners have experienced both hard-fought contests (such as John Cook's long road to victory in the six-hole sudden-death playoff in 1983) and easy rides (such as Johnny Palmer's walk to an 11-stroke win in 1952). But usually spectators have had the chance to watch the world's best golfers duel it out over at least 72 holes to claim the victory.

As of 2003, 72 individuals have held the title. One player, Leo Diegel, took the title an unprecedented four times, and it was this four-time victory that finally assisted Diegel into the World Golf Hall of Fame in 2003. Only three others have won it three times: Tommy Armour (1927, 1930, 1934), Sam Snead (1938, 1940, 1941) and Lee Trevino (1971, 1977, 1979). Repeat winners are not so uncommon, from Charles and Albert Murray (1906, 1911 and 1908, 1913, respectively), Karl Keffer (1909, 1914), J.D. Edgar (1919, 1920), Harry Cooper (1932, 1937), Jim Ferrier (1950, 1951), Doug Ford (1959, 1963), Bruce Lietzke (1978, 1982), Greg Norman (1984, 1992), Curtis Strange (1985, 1987), Steve Jones (1989, 1997) and Nick Price (1991, 1994). But of these, only Edgar, Snead and Ferrier have successfully defended their titles. The honour of the longest gap between victories (eight years) goes to Greg Norman and Steve Jones. And Jones won it on two different courses for two different trophies in his eight-year stretch.

Although amateur competitors have a long history in the tournament, and a few have managed to come in second (such as Tom Reith in 1906, the legendary Bobby Jones in 1919 and an amateur Tommy Armour in 1920), only one has captured the title—Doug Sanders.

Two individuals have won the Triple Crown—the Canadian Open in conjunction with the national championships of Britain and the United States in a single year—Lee Trevino and Tiger Woods.

The youngest champion was Albert Murray, just 20 years old when he took the title at his brother's home, The Royal Montreal Golf Club, while the oldest winner to take the title did so in its 99th year; Bob Tway was 44 when he defeated 43-year-old Brad Faxon over three hotly contested playoff holes.

Although the last Canadian to win the title was Saskatchewan's Pat Fletcher in 1954, many Canadians have challenged for the title in the 50 years since. Such outstanding players as Stan Leonard, Al Balding, George Knudson, Dave Barr and, most recently, Mike Weir have teed it up and made a run for national honour. Cruel luck, a moment's falter, and another non-Canadian is crowned champion.

— 1904 —

JOHN H. OKE

▸ Born: Northam, England, 1880

▸ Professional at (Royal) Ottawa Golf Club 1904–05

▸ Worked at Royal North Devon Club and served as assistant to J.H. Taylor (of the Great Triumvirate) at Mid-Surrey Golf Club

▸ Returned to England in 1905, then emigrated to U.S. in 1918

— 1905 —

GEORGE CUMMING

▸ Born: Bridge of Weir, Scotland, May 20, 1879

▸ Professional at the Toronto Golf Club from 1900 until his death in 1950

▸ Apprenticed to Andrew Fergan, Glasgow Golf Club

▸ Other showings in Canadian Open: runner-up in 1906, 1907, 1909, 1914

▸ Also won CPGA Championship, 1914

▸ 1905 U.S. Open: tied lowest 18-hole score for eighth place

▸ Dean of Canadian Professionals

— 1906 & 1911 —

CHARLES MURRAY

▸ Born: Nottingham, England, 1882

▸ Professional at The Royal Montreal Golf Club from 1905 until his death in 1938

▸ Immigrated in 1880s with family, settled in Toronto and trained under George Cumming

▸ Also won CPGA Championship, 1912; Quebec Open, 1909, 1911, 1912, 1913, 1914, 1921, 1922, 1923, 1924

▸ Other showings in Canadian Opens: tied for runner-up, 1920, 15 top tens

— 1907 —

PERCY BARRETT

▸ Born: Huddersfield, England, 1880

▸ Professional at the Lambton Golf and Country Club from 1903–14, then at Weston (1915–22) Uplands (1923) and Lakeshore (1924–26), all in the Toronto area.

▸ Protégé of Harry Vardon (of the Great Triumvirate) at Ganton, England

▸ Showing in Canadian Opens: runner-up, 1904, 1905; four other third-place finishes before 1911 (all of which earned him a total of $400)

▸ Also won CPGA Championship, 1923, 1925, as pro at Weston Golf and Country Club

▸ Died suddenly in 1927

— 1908 & 1913 —

ALBERT MURRAY

- Born: Nottingham, England, September 3, 1887
- Professional at the Outremont Golf Club, Montreal
- Immigrated to Canada with family in the 1880s
- Trained under George Cumming
- Youngest winner of the Open (20 years of age)
- Also won CPGA Championship, 1924; Quebec Open, 1930
- Opened Canada's first indoor golf school and was also a golf architect
- Died 1974

— 1909 & 1914 —

KARL KEFFER

- Born: Tottenham, Ontario, 1882
- Professional at Royal Ottawa Golf Club 1911–45
- Trained under George Cumming
- Other showings in Candian Open: Runner-up, 1919, tied with Bobby Jones
- Also won Manitoba Open, 1919; Quebec Open, 1927
- Only Canadian-born player to win the Canadian Open
- Service in WWI apparently hampered his playing ability

DANIEL KENNY

- ▸ Born: North Berwick, Scotland, 1882
- ▸ First American to win the Canadian Open
- ▸ Played in five Canadian Opens between 1907 and 1921
- ▸ Professional at the Buffalo Golf and Country Club

GEORGE SARGENT

- ▸ Born: Dorking, England, 1882
- ▸ Professional at the (Royal) Ottawa Golf Club, 1906–08
- ▸ Protégé of Harry Vardon (of the Great Triumvirate)
- ▸ Won U.S. Open, 1909, with record-breaking 209
- ▸ President of PGA of America, 1921–26
- ▸ Introduced motion picture swing analysis in 1930
- ▸ Died 1962

— 1919 & 1920 —

J. D. (JOHN DOUGLAS) EDGAR

- Born: Newcastle-on-Tyne, England September 30, 1884
- Professional at Druid's Hill Club, Atlanta, Georgia
- Won French Open, 1914
- Wrote *The Gate to Golf*, a golf instruction manual with teaching aid
- Won the 1919 Canadian Open with a record 278 strokes
- Died 1921

— 1921 —

W. H. TROVINGER

- Born: Michigan, 1890
- Began golf at 11 years old at Kent Golf Club, Michigan
- Professional at Bloomfield Hills Country Club, Birmingham, Michigan, and Spring Lake Country Club, Grand Haven, Michigan
- Finished third in the Michigan Open, 1921

— 1922 —

A. A. (ANDREW ALBERT) WATROUS

▶ Born: Yonkers, New York, 1899
▶ Professional at the Redford Country Club, Detroit, Michigan
▶ Michigan Open champion six times between 1926 and 1949
▶ Michigan PGA champion nine times
▶ Runner-up in British Open, 1926; member of Ryder Cup team, 1927, 1929;
▶ Won the U.S. Seniors, 1950 & 1951
▶ Died 1983

— 1923 —

CLARENCE W. HACKNEY

▶ Born: Carnoustie, Scotland, date unknown
▶ Professional at the Country Club of Atlantic City, New Jersey

— 1924, 1925, 1928 & 1929 —

LEO DIEGEL

▸ Born: Detroit, Michigan, April 27, 1899

▸ Won PGA championship 1928, 1929

▸ Member of first four Ryder Cup teams

▸ Gave the name to a putting stroke known as "Diegeling"

▸ Wrote an instructional book called *Nine Bad Shots of Golf*

▸ Instrumental in establishing the Tucson Open

▸ Died 1951

— 1926 —

MacDONALD SMITH

▸ Born: Carnoustie, Scotland, 1890

▸ Finished third in U.S. Open, 1910; runner-up, 1930

▸ Won Western Open, 1912, 1925

▸ At the time considered the best player never to have won the British or U.S. Opens

▸ Died 1949

— 1927, 1930 & 1934 —

TOMMY ARMOUR

▸ Born: Edinburgh, Scotland, September 24, 1894

▸ Pro at Congressional Country Club, Washington, DC, 1926–29;

▸ Tam O'Shanter Golf Club, Detroit, Michigan, 1929–31; Medinah Country Club, Chicago, Illinois, 1932–43

▸ Won U.S. Open, 1927; PGA Championship, 1930; British Open, 1931

▸ Wrote *A Round of Golf with Tommy Armour, Classic Golf Tips* and *How to Play Your Best Golf All the Time*

▸ Died 1968

— 1931 —

WALTER HAGEN

▸ Born: Rochester, New York, December 21, 1892

▸ Won U.S. Open, 1914, 1919; British Open, 1922, 1924, 1928, 1929; PGA Championship, 1921, 1924, 1925, 1926, 1927

▸ Known for his colourful approach to the game

▸ Wrote *The Haig*

▸ Credo: "You're only here for a short visit. Don't hurry. Don't worry. And be sure to smell the flowers along the way."

▸ Died October 5, 1969

HARRY COOPER

- ▸ Born: Leatherhead, England, August 4, 1904
- ▸ Immigrated as a boy to Canada, where his father was steward of the Hamilton Golf and Country Club
- ▸ Grew up in Texas
- ▸ Won Los Angeles $10,000 Open championship in 1926
- ▸ Lost U.S. Open in playoff with Armour in 1927
- ▸ Held record for shooting 60 over 18 holes
- ▸ Nickname: "Lighthorse"
- ▸ Died 1999

JOE KIRKWOOD

- ▸ Born: Sydney, Australia, 1897
- ▸ Won Australian Open, 1920; New Zealand Open, 1920; Australian PGA, 1920
- ▸ Beat Harry Vardon in England in 1921
- ▸ Trick-shot artist
- ▸ Died 1970

— 1935 —

GENE KUNES

▸ Born: Erie, Pennsylvania, 1908

▸ Professional at South Hill Country Club Golf, Norristown, Pennsylvania

▸ Also won Maryland Open, 1935; Pennsylvania Open, 1941

▸ Played in eight Canadian Opens between 1930 and 1964

— 1936 —

LAWSON LITTLE

▸ Born: Newport, Rhode Island, June 23, 1910

▸ Great amateur player, won U.S. and British Amateur titles, 1934, 1935; U.S. Open, 1940

▸ Died 1968

— 1938, 1940, 1941 —

SAM SNEAD

- ▶ Born: Hot Springs, West Virginia, May 27, 1912
- ▶ Also won PGA Championship, 1942, 1949, 1951; Masters, 1949, 1952, 1954; 82 wins on PGA Tour
- ▶ Runner-up at 1969 Open at the age of 57
- ▶ Nickname: "Slammin' Sam"
- ▶ Died May 23, 2002

— 1939 —

HAROLD McSPADEN

- ▶ Born: Rosedale, Kansas, July 21, 1908
- ▶ Not accepted into the forces during WWII, McSpaden and his best friend on the Tour, Byron Nelson, did more than 100 exhibition matches to raise money for the war effort
- ▶ Had 17 career victories; placed second on the 1944 money list; had three consecutive second-place finishes to Nelson during Byron's 11-victory run in 1945
- ▶ Nicknames: "Jug" and, with Nelson, "The Gold Dust Twins"
- ▶ Died April 1996

— 1942 —

CRAIG WOOD

▸ Born: Lake Placid, New York, 1901

▸ Ryder Cup team member, 1931, 1933, 1935

▸ Died 1968

— 1945 —

BYRON NELSON

▸ Born: Fort Worth, Texas, February 4, 1912

▸ Won Masters, 1937, 1942; PGA Championship 1940, 1945; U.S. Open, 1939

▸ Recorded 11 consecutive victories in 1945

▸ Made 115 consecutive cuts

— 1946 —

GEORGE FAZIO

- Born: Philadelphia, Pennsylvania, 1911
- Semi-prominent professional during 1940s and 1950s
- Became a golf course architect in the 1960s and designed such courses as Pinehurst No. 6 and Juniper Hill, Florida
- Uncle to famed golf course architect Tom Fazio
- Died 1986

— 1947 —

BOBBY LOCKE

- Born: Germiston, South Africa, 1917
- Served in South African Air Force during WWII
- Won South African Open, 1938, 1939, 1940
- Won the Harry Vardon Trophy, 1946, and seven titles (four in five starts) in the U.S. and Canada in 1947
- In two and a half years in North America, won 11 of 59 tournaments and was runner-up 15 times
- Also won British Open 1949, 1950, 1952, 1957

— 1948 —

CHUCK CONGDON

▸ Born: Tacoma, Washington

▸ Professional at Tacoma Golf and
  Country Club, 1935–65

▸ Won Washington Open 1939, 1947, 1950,
  1952, 1962

▸ Founder and president of Pacific
  Northwest Section of PGA

▸ Died 1965

— 1949 —

E.J. (DUTCH) HARRISON

▸ Born: Arkansas City, Arkansas,
  March 29, 1910

▸ Won 15 events between 1937 and 1958;
  Western Open, 1953; Bing Crosby
  Pro-Am, 1954

▸ Won U.S. National Senior Open, 1962,
  1963, 1964, 1965

▸ Regular on Ryder Cup team

▸ Died June 19, 1982

JIM FERRIER

▶ Born: Manly, Australia, February 24, 1915

▶ First Australian to win a major

▶ Won five of six New South Wales Opens between 1933 and 1938; Australian Open, 1938, 1939

▶ On U.S. Tour 18 times; won PGA Championship, 1947

▶ Died June 13, 1986

JOHNNY PALMER

▶ Born: El Dorado, North Carolina, 1918

▶ Won Nashville Invitational, 1946; Western Open, 1947; Houston Open, 1948; World Championship of Golf, 1949

— 1953 —

DAVE DOUGLAS

- Won Shell Houston Open, 1955
- Member of Ryder Cup team, 1953
- Played in eight Canadian Opens between 1948 and 1956

— 1954 —

PAT FLETCHER

- Born: Clacton-on-Sea, England, June 18, 1916
- Professional at the Saskatoon Golf and Country Club 1946–56; The Royal Montreal Golf Club, 1956–75
- Immigrated to Canada at four years of age, raised in Victoria, British Columbia
- Won CPGA Championship, 1952; Saskatchewan Open, 1947, 1948, 1951; Quebec Spring Open, 1956, 1957
- Died in 1985

— 1955 —

ARNOLD PALMER

▸ Born: Latrobe, Pennsylvania, September 10, 1929

▸ U.S. Amateur champion, 1954

▸ Won 62 PGA Tour events, including four Masters, two British Opens, a U.S. Open and 29 tournaments between 1960 and 1963; 10 Champions Tour events and 11 other international tournaments

▸ Member of six Ryder Cup teams

▸ Won six Canada Cups, playing with Sam Snead and Jack Nicklaus

▸ First player to reach US$1 million in career earnings (1968); led the PGA Tour in earnings four times

— 1956 —

DOUG SANDERS

▸ Born: Cedartown, Georgia, July 24, 1933

▸ Turned pro after winning Canadian Open, 1956

▸ Won Western Open, 1958

▸ Won 17 other PGA Tour Events

▸ Member of the 1967 Ryder Cup Team

— 1957 —

GEORGE BAYER

▸ Born: Bremerton, Washington, 1926

▸ Played for the NFL Redskins, 1949

▸ Took up professional golf at 29 years of age

▸ Also won Mayfair Inn Open, 1958; St. Petersburg Open, 1960

▸ Died March 23, 2003

— 1958 —

WESLEY ELLIS JR.

▸ Won the Texas Open, 1966

▸ Played in five Canadian Opens, between 1958 and 1970, winning $6,632 in total

— 1959, 1963 —

DOUG FORD

▸ Born: West Haven, Connecticut, August 6, 1922

▸ Turned pro in 1949

▸ Won PGA Championship, 1955; Masters, 1957; 15 other Tour events

▸ Member of Ryder Cup team, 1955, 1957, 1959, 1961

— 1960 —

ART WALL, JR.

▸ Born: Honesdale, PA, November 25, 1923

▸ Masters champion, Crosby, Vardon Trophy, 1959

▸ Won 12 PGA Tour events, including the Greater Hartford Open in 1966, and the Greater Milwakee Open in 1975—at 51, the oldest PGA Tour winner

▸ Fighting Billy Casper for the Canadian Open championship in 1967 in Montreal, Wall birdied the 16th with a 20-foot putt. As he walked to the 17th tee, one of the spectators said, "Way to go, Art. Let's get two more birdies and then you can give us a big smile." Art didn't break stride as he turned to the man and said "Sir, if this were a smiling contest, I wouldn't have entered.'"

▸ Died October 31, 2001

JACKY CUPIT

▸ Born: Longview, Texas, February 1, 1938

▸ Won four PGA Tour events

▸ Recently the professional at The Links at Lands End, Texas

TED KROLL

▸ Born: New Hartford, New York, August 14, 1919

▸ Awarded three Purple Hearts during WWII

▸ Joined PGA Tour in 1949

▸ Won Greater Hartford Open, 1952

▸ Died April 25, 2002

— 1964 —

KELVIN NAGLE

▸ Born: North Sydney, Australia, December 21, 1920

▸ Won (with Peter Thomson) the Canada Cup (now called the World Cup), 1954, 1959; British Open, 1960

▸ Also won New Zealand Open and New Zealand PGA nine times each

— 1965 —

GENE LITTLER

▸ Born: San Diego, California, July 21, 1930

▸ U.S. Amateur champion, 1953

▸ Won 1954 San Diego Open as an amateur

▸ Won 29 PGA Tour events, including U.S. Open, 1961

▸ Member of seven Ryder Cup teams

▸ Winner of eight Champions Tour events

▸ Inducted into the World Golf Hall of Fame in 1990

▸ Nicknamed "Gene the Machine" because of his smooth tempo swinging the golf club

DON MASSENGALE

▸ Born: Jacksboro, Texas, April 23 1937,

▸ Played in five Canadian Opens between 1960 and 1970

▸ Won a total of $22,981

BILLY CASPER

▸ Born: San Diego, California, June 24, 1931

▸ Won 51 PGA Tour events, including U.S. Open, 1959, 1966; Masters, 1970

▸ Member of seven Ryder Cup teams

▸ Won nine Champions Tour events

▸ Second player to reach US$1 million in career earnings (1970); leading money winner on PGA Tour twice (1966, 1968)

▸ PGA Tour Player of the Year, 1966, 1970

— 1968 —

BOB CHARLES

▶ Born: Carterton, New Zealand, March 14, 1936

▶ Won six PGA Tour events, including British Open, 1963; 21 other tournament wins worldwide

▶ Won 23 Champions Tour events

▶ Member of nine New Zealand World Cup teams

▶ Only left-handed golfer to win a major before Mike Weir won the Masters in 2003

▶ Does everything right-handed except games requiring two hands

— 1969 —

TOMMY AARON

▶ Born: Gainsville, Georgia, February 22, 1937

▶ Won three PGA Tour events, including the Masters, 1973

▶ Member of two Ryder Cup teams

▶ One Champions Tour win

▶ Made the cut at the 2000 Masters (at 63, the oldest player ever to make the cut)

KERMIT ZARLEY

▸ Born: Seattle, Washington,
September 29, 1941

▸ NCAA individual champion while at
the University of Houston, 1962

▸ Two PGA Tour wins

▸ One Champions Tour win

▸ Co-founded the PGA Tour Bible Study
group in 1965

LEE TREVINO

▸ Born: Dallas, Texas, December 1, 1939

▸ Spent four years in the U.S. Marine Corps

▸ Won 29 PGA Tour events, including six
majors: U.S. Open, 1968 (his first Tour
win), 1971; British Open, 1971, 1972; PGA
Championship, 1974, 1984; Canadian
PGA champion, 1983

▸ Member of six Ryder Cup teams

▸ Won 29 Champions Tour events

▸ Won five Vardon trophies for lowest
scoring average on Tour

GAY BREWER, JR.

▸ Born: Middletown, Ohio, March 19, 1932

▸ Won Carling Open, 1961

▸ Masters champion, 1967

▸ Member of Ryder Cup team, 1967, 1971

TOM WEISKOPF

▸ Born: Massillon, Ohio, November 9, 1942

▸ Won 16 PGA Tour events, including British Open, 1973

▸ Won five tournaments within an eight-week span in 1973

▸ Four-time runner-up at the Masters

▸ Member of two Ryder Cup teams

▸ Four Champions Tour victories

BOBBY NICHOLS

▸ Born: Louisville, Kentucky, April 14, 1936

▸ Won 1964 PGA Championship

▸ Eleven other PGA Tour events

▸ One Champions Tour victory

▸ Member of the 1967 Ryder Cup Team

▸ Recipient of the 1962 Ben Hogan Award

JERRY PATE

▸ Born: Macon, Georgia, September 16, 1953

▸ U.S. Amateur champion, 1974

▸ Won eight PGA Tour events, including U.S. Open, 1976

▸ Member of Ryder Cup team, 1981

▸ Claimed the 1982 Tournament Players Championship

▸ Rookie earnings of US$153,102 in 1976 were the most ever until Hal Sutton broke the mark in 1982

▸ Always marks his ball with coin on tails

— 1978, 1982 —

BRUCE LIETZKE

- Born: Kansas City, Kansas, July 18, 1951
- Won 13 PGA Tour events
- Won four tournaments twice, including the Canadian Open
- Seven Champions Tour victories
- Member of Ryder Cup team, 1981
- The only player in the field at all three tournaments at which a player shot a 59: the 1977 Danny Thomas Memphis Classic (Al Geiberger), 1991 Las Vegas Invitational (Chip Beck) and 1999 Bob Hope Chrysler Classic (David Duval)

— 1980 —

BOB GILDER

- Born: Corvallis, Oregon, December 31, 1950
- Six PGA Tour and seven Champions Tour victories
- Member of Ryder Cup team, 1983
- The highlight of his 1983 Westchester Classic victory was a third-round double eagle on the 509-yard 18th hole. A fairway marker commemorates the feat and marks the exact spot where he hit his 3-wood

— 1981 —

PETER OOSTERHUIS

▸ Born: England, May 3, 1948

▸ Turned professional 1968

▸ Won 19 international events

▸ Led British Order of Merit, 1971, 1972, 1973, 1974

▸ Runner-up, British Open, 1974, 1982

▸ Canadian Open his only win on the PGA Tour

— 1983 —

JOHN COOK

▸ Born: Toledo, Ohio, October 2, 1957

▸ 1978 U.S. Amateur champion

▸ Won 11 PGA Tour events, including his first, in a five-man playoff at the Bing Crosby National Pro-Am, 1981

▸ Won three times and finished third in earnings in 1992

▸ Won at least one event for three straight years, 1996–98

GREG NORMAN

▶ Born: Mt. Isa, Queensland, Australia, February 10, 1955

▶ Won 20 PGA Tour events, including British Open, 1986, 1993; 66 international victories

▶ Finished as runner-up eight times at a major

▶ First player to earn US$1 million four times (1990, 1993, 1994, 1995); finished in the top 10 on the money list nine times; in 1996, became the first player to surpass US$10 million in earnings

▶ Nickname: "The Shark"

CURTIS STRANGE

▶ Born: Norfolk, Virginia, January 30, 1955

▶ Won the NCAA championship while attending Wake Forest University, 1974; Won 17 PGA Tour events, including back-to-back U.S. Opens in 1988 and 1989

▶ First player to surpass US$1 million in a season (1988); topped the season money list three times

▶ At least one victory for seven consecutive years, 1983 to 1989

▶ Member of five Ryder Cup teams

— 1986 —

BOB MURPHY

- ▸ Born: Brooklyn, New York, February 14, 1943
- ▸ U.S. Amateur champion, 1965
- ▸ NCAA champion, 1966
- ▸ Won five PGA Tour events
- ▸ Earnings of US$105,595 in 1968 at the time a record for a first-year PGA Tour player
- ▸ 11 Champions Tour victories
- ▸ Member of Ryder Cup team, 1975
- ▸ Received the 1996 Ben Hogan Award from the Golf Writers Association of America for his comeback from arthritis

— 1988 —

KEN GREEN

- ▸ Born: Danbury, Connecticut, July 23, 1958
- ▸ Started playing golf at age 12 in Honduras, where his father was principal of the American School and the only choices for sports were golf or soccer
- ▸ Won five PGA Tour events
- ▸ Member of Ryder Cup team, 1989

— 1989, 1997 —

STEVE JONES

▸ Born: Artesia, New Mexico, December 27, 1958

▸ Won eight PGA Tour events, including U.S. Open, 1996

▸ Spent nearly three years off the Tour due to ligament and joint damage to left ring finger suffered in 1991; completed comeback in 1996 to become first sectional qualifier to win U.S. Open since Jerry Pate in 1976

— 1990 —

WAYNE LEVI

▸ Born: Little Falls, New York, February 22, 1952

▸ Won 12 PGA Tour events

▸ Won the 1982 Hawaiian Open with an orange golf ball, the first player to win with a ball that wasn't white

▸ PGA Tour Player of the Year, 1990, after winning four times and becoming just the fifth player to earn more than US$1 million in a season

NICK PRICE

▸ Born: Durban, South Africa, January 28, 1957

▸ 18 PGA Tour victories, including PGA Championship, 1992, 1994; British Open, 1994

▸ One of only three players in the 1990s to win two major titles in the same season, joining Nick Faldo (1990) and Mark O'Meara (1998)

▸ Member of four Presidents Cup teams

▸ Along with Tiger Woods, his 15 victories were the most by any player in the 1990s

▸ One of only seven players since 1945 to capture consecutive majors, joining Ben Hogan, Jack Nicklaus, Arnold Palmer, Lee Trevino, Tom Watson and Tiger Woods

▸ Finished in the top 50 on the money list for 17 consecutive seasons, 1984 to 2002

DAVID FROST

▸ Born: Cape Town, South Africa, September 11, 1959

▸ 10 PGA Tour victories

▸ 12 international victories

▸ 2 Presidents Cup Teams

▸ In 1994, established 300-acre vineyard with brother Michael in South Africa

MARK O'MEARA

▸ Born: Goldsboro, North Carolina, January 13, 1957

▸ U.S. Amateur champion, 1979

▸ Won 16 PGA Tour victories, including Masters, 1998; British Open, 1998

▸ PGA Tour Player of the Year, 1998

▸ Oldest player to win two major championships in the same year

▸ Won at Augusta on his 15th try—the most for any first-time champion

▸ Six of his victories have come at pro-am events

▸ Member of five Ryder Cup teams

DUDLEY HART

▸ Born: Rochester, New York, August 4, 1968

▸ Two PGA Tour wins

▸ Father of triplets and a hockey fan who has season's tickets for the Florida Panthers

— 1998 —

BILLY ANDRADE

▶ Born: Bristol, Rhode Island,
January 25, 1964

▶ Member of NCAA Championship team
from Wake Forest University, 1986

▶ Four PGA Tour wins

▶ In the closest race ever for the top 30,
season earnings of US$665,602 missed
qualifying by US$5 in 1997

▶ Became the first player in six years to
win first two Tour titles in consecutive
weeks in June 1991

— 1999 —

HAL SUTTON

▶ Born: Shreveport, Louisiana,
April 28, 1958

▶ U.S. Amateur champion, 1980

▶ Won 14 PGA events, including PGA
Championship, 1983

▶ Won seven times in his 20s, once in his
30s and six times in his 40s

▶ Member of four Ryder Cup teams

— 2000 —

TIGER WOODS

▸ Born: Cypress, California, December 30, 1975

▸ To date, has won 39 PGA Tour events, including eight major championships: Masters, 1997, 2001, 2002; British Open, 2000; PGA championship, 1999, 2000; U.S. Open, 2000, 2001

▸ PGA Tour Player of the year six times

▸ Led the Tour in season earnings five out of six years

▸ Holds 72-hole record at Masters, British Open and U.S. Open

▸ In 2000, won three consecutive majors, nine times overall, set the single-season earnings mark of US$9,188,321 and his non-adjusted scoring average of 68.17 was the best in the history of the game

▸ With his Masters victory in 2001, became the first player to hold all four professional major titles at once

— 2001 —

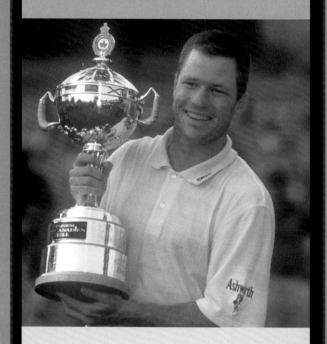

SCOTT VERPLANK

▸ Born: Dallas, Texas, July 9, 1964

▸ U.S. Amateur champion, 1984

▸ Won the 1985 Western Open as an amateur, the first amateur to win a PGA Tour event in 29 years (since Doug Sanders at 1956 Canadian Open)

▸ NCAA champion, 1986

▸ Time between his 1988 Buick Open win and his victory at the 2000 Reno-Tahoe Open (12 years, 27 days) is the fifth longest in PGA Tour history

▸ Won medallist honours at 1997 PGA Tour Qualifying Tournament

▸ Finished 18th on the money list in 1998, the highest by a Q-School grad since John Daly was 17th in 1991

▸ Member of Ryder Cup team, 2002

— 2002 —

JOHN ROLLINS

▶ Born: Richmond, Virginia, June 25, 1975

▶ Virginia State Amateur champion, 1996, 1997

▶ Finished sixth on the Nationwide Tour money list in 2001 to ensure a return to the PGA Tour, where he finished 13th on the money list in 2002, the best finish in the following season by a Nationwide Tour grad since David Duval finished ninth in 1995

— 2003 —

BOB TWAY

▶ Born: Oklahoma City, Oklahoma, May 4, 1959

▶ Three-time All-American at Oklahoma State University and member of two national championship teams, 1978, 1980

▶ To date, has won eight PGA Tour events, including PGA Championship, 1986

▶ Finished outside the top 100 money winners just four times in 16 years on the Tour

THE PRIZE

The Rivermead Challenge Cup rotated, primarily across the border to the United States, for each year's sojourn at the winner's club—with the exception of 1933, when the trophy made it to the border and no further. It was held at the border at Buffalo, New York, for the year of Australian Joe Kirkwood's championship. Kirkwood was serving as the professional at a club in Chicago, but the trophy never did make it to the display case.

The first Canadian Open was not graced with a trophy. In 1904, the Open was a mere one-day event, played over 36 holes, immediately following the Canadian Amateur championship. The winner was awarded a cash prize of $60 and the RCGA medal, inscribed to reflect winning the Open for that year.

To put this in some context, the Royal Canadian Golf Association conducting the event was but nine years new. The Association was growing but still didn't have staff of any kind. Its president was chosen from the club that was to host the coming year's national events; its funding depended on a $10 annual fee from member clubs; and with only somewhere around 70 clubs in the country, the young Association was hardly wealthy.

Following the success of the 1904 event, the organization decided to continue the championship. For the next seven years, it would continue on the course where the Amateur was played. The purse increased slightly, from a total of $170 in 1904 to $225 in 1905 and $245 in 1907. In 1907, the event was also extended to two days and 72 holes. The Open first separated from the Amateur championship in 1912. Yet throughout those years, the RCGA retained its gold medal for first place and a silver medal for second.

When the championship for 1920 was awarded to the relatively new Rivermead Golf Club in Ottawa, enthusiasm was enormous at the host club. In addition to raising a further $100 for the first prize (for a total of $300), the club sought a trophy that would epitomize the Open and initiated the use of the Rivermead Challenge Cup. When 1919 champion J.D. Edgar repeated his win the next year, he became this new trophy's first recipient. Formidable names in golf history—Tommy Armour, Walter Hagen, Leo Diegel—were later presented with the Rivermead Cup, along with a growing purse.

With the growing popularity of the professional golfers' tour of championships, the demand for a bigger purse began to affect the RCGA. After the introduction of entrance fees for spectators in the early 1920s, the Open took on a larger role as a means of sustenance for both itself and the association. The quality of the field not only reflected the quality of the championship, it also played a role in the increasingly important gate income.

In 1936, the RCGA took its first steps into what was becoming an established part of professional sports when it took on a sponsor.

The Seagram Company saw the tournament's value in promoting its product and boosted the purse to $3,000. To recognize the new sponsor's support, the Association agreed to replace the Rivermead Cup with the Seagram Gold Cup.

First presented in 1936 to Lawson Little, the Seagram Gold Cup was designed to incorporate images of Canada, from the maple leaf and the beaver to the gold-plated finish. Rather than the customary inscription of the winner's name on the trophy, the Seagram Gold Cup incorporated a hollow base where a specially crafted box holds a scroll with the names of the champions recorded in illuminated calligraphy. Names such as Sam Snead, Byron Nelson and Arnold Palmer are recorded on this scroll, which was used for the next 35 years. When the Seagram company felt it had to pull out of its 35-year sponsorship, the Seagram Cup was presented for the last time to Kermit Zarley, champion of the 1970 Open.

When a new sponsor, the Imperial Tobacco Company of Canada, naturally wanted to make its own mark on the tournament, another trophy was created. Initially called the Peter Jackson Trophy and later the du Maurier Trophy, the new award was unique in the golf world. Again a special base was created, but the award itself was an Inuit sculpture that the winner could keep. Champions including Lee Trevino, Greg Norman, Nick Price, and Bruce Lietzke and David Frost have a soapstone carving from the Canadian north in their homes.

In 1994, the Open faced yet another change in the championship trophy. Tobacco companies were no longer permitted to advertise sponsorships, so the RCGA sought a new partner for the ever-growing tournament. With a purse now reaching into the millions, Bell Canada accepted the challenge. Along with the sponsorship that would underwrite the big bucks required to maintain a high profile on the Tour, the Open championship would become the Bell Canadian Open. Thus, while it bore the new name of the tournament, the trophy was no longer the sponsor's most identifying feature.

For these reasons, the RCGA sought out a new trophy that would withstand the changing nature of sponsorships. The Bell Canadian Open Trophy reaches back to the origins of the game. Sitting on a base of Canadian Maple, it is made of sterling silver and inscribed with the names of the champions from 1904 to today.

The Seagram Gold Cup also began the all but steady trip south of the border so the champion could showcase it in his home or home club. While the winner had to return the Gold Cup in time for the next championship, he was also presented with a miniature cup to commemorate his victory. But the Seagram Cup was not without its own adventures. It was held hostage in the 1949 divorce settlement of champion Dutch Harrison when his estranged wife claimed the trophy as part of his assets. A judge ruled that it was indeed not part of Harrison's assets and it was released just in time to be shipped to Royal Montreal for the 1950 Open.

The base of the du Maurier Trophy incorporates the maple leaf, crossed clubs and silver plates to bear the inscriptions. The trophy itself didn't have to travel across border on a yearly basis, while the champion's award was a unique piece of art— an award that some champions have said is their favourite.

The flags of each province
and territory in Canada
surround the lip of the Bell
Canadian Open Trophy itself,
while the lid features a map of
the nation and the maple leaf.
The RCGA crest crowns it all to
identify the organization,
now more than 100 years
old, that has conducted
the championship
since 1904.

THE VOLUNTEERS

Volunteers have been a fundamental part of the Open. Today you can find them walking the course, reporting to the scoring centres, carrying leader boards and working in admissions, hospitality, player services, transportation and a host of other areas.

ABOVE LEFT Rod McIsaac wasn't a volunteer, but he was a significant player in Canadian Open history. It was McIsaac who attended the 1972 Open at Cherry Hill—and couldn't see the play for the crowds. And that's what provoked him to approach the RCGA about redesigning a course he owned in Oakville as a permanent home for the Open.

ABOVE RIGHT Richard Grimm (pictured), along with Bruce Forbes, John Marshall and the folks from Imperial Tobacco, made the move to Glen Abbey happen. Grimm is an example of a volunteer extraordinaire. He first served the Open as club chairman at Mississaugua in 1965 and continued through to the 1980s, when he became tournament director and later the Commissioner of the Canadian Tour.

What would the Open be without its volunteers? In fact, how would any professional golf tournament exist without the thousands of volunteers and the tens of thousand of hours they commit to the championships?

The first Canadian Open would never have been played without the work of volunteers, as the Royal Canadian Golf Association did not have paid staff in 1904. And even as the Open grew, the association was conservative, first hiring one part-time person in 1919 and not expanding to two until the 1940s. By 1967, Canada's Centennial year, only three people were committed on a full-time basis to operate the Open. Meanwhile, crews of up to 2,000 volunteers from all walks of life commit to one week's full service, plus countless meetings throughout the year, to run the championship.

Of these many tremendous and committed individuals, a few go even further. The committee chairs work throughout the year leading up to the championship to orchestrate their roles as transportation,

player services, marshals, security, corporate hospitality, admissions and medical staff, while other committees take on the operations of the tournament itself.

The board of the RCGA is another very significant element of the machine that presents the Bell Canadian Open. Because the association conducts the Open each year, its governors are responsible for the policies and objectives of the association's operations. Leading up to and during the tournament, these individuals don their volunteer hats to become starters, scorers and rules officials, serving the Open with the same commitment they give the other 20 RCGA-conducted events during the year.

ABOVE The 2000 tournament, when Glen Abbey served its last year as the "permanent home" of the Canadian Open, was the end of an era in many ways. Over the 23 years the Open had been held primarily in Oakville, where a tremendous team of volunteers had been assembled. Here, the chairpeople for the 2000 Open gather on the steps of Golf House, the historic abbey responsible for the course's name.

THE MEDIA
and THE OPEN

Before the advent of regular coast-to-coast telecasts of the Open, fans would tune into the radio to follow the play-by-play action. Here a CBC Radio crew covers the 1960 Open at St. George's Golf and Country Club with on air personality Bob MacLaughlin (left).

ABOVE Television camera crews following the leader on the links are a regular sight at the Open today, like this CTV crew in the 1990s. One of the advantages of the move to Glen Abbey in 1977 was the ability to have permanently installed cables for TV broadcasting.

From a single-line entry in the daily newspaper to television stations 100% dedicated to golf and coverage of all four days of the Open championship, the media have been a partner every step of the way in the 100 years since the first Canadian Open.

As the Open Golf Championship of Canada became a more established tournament, more and more print space was dedicated to both promoting the tournament and recapping the results. By 1915, Canadian golf was so popular that a monthly magazine, *Canadian Golfer,* was established and provided an invaluable tool in the days before regular radio and television coverage. Dedicating up to 20 pages to reporting the events of the tournament, this publication gives today's reader an intimate knowledge of yesterday's competitions.

The introduction of radio coverage allowed golf lovers to share the excitement even if they couldn't be present. CFRB and CBC both began daily broadcasts of the Open in the 1930s. Onsite personalities would walk the course with the leaders, providing shot-by-shot editorials and inspiring the ever-growing interest in the championship as we swung to the popularization of professional players.

But the advent of television has had the most significant impact on the game and the PGA Tour. The first coast-to-coast telecast of the Canadian Open, in 1955, brought one of the most endearing personalities in professional golf into living rooms across Canada when the 24-year-old Arnold Palmer won his first PGA Tour victory and inspired people to pick up their clubs and hit the golf course for themselves.

The other effect of television on golf, and of golf on television, involves the technical demands of covering a game played over 150 acres and 18 holes, with 150 potential champions. Indeed, the requirements of telecasting have had far-reaching effects on the very nature of golf. And the benefits and popularity of the game, partly inspired by televising the game, have had significant effects on the broadcasters. The revenues from television have had a huge impact on the role of sponsorship and the players' purses.

The Internet has added a fourth element to the traditional media coverage. You can now follow a tournament leader board half a world away live on your home computer and "chat" with others online who share golf's singular passion.

ABOVE Radio stations across Canada broadcast the Open—right through to the 1970s.

CANADIAN OPEN CHAMPIONSHIP

PRIOR TO 1936 ....RIVERMEAD CUP
1936—1970 ....SEAGRAM GOLD CUP
1971—1983 ....PETER JACKSON TROPHY
1984—1993 ....du MAURIER TROPHY
SINCE 1994 ....BELL CANADIAN OPEN TROPHY

YEAR	WINNER	SCORE	RUNNER-UP	SCORE	COURSE AND VENUE
1904	J.H. Oke, *Ottawa, Ont.*	156	P.F. Barrett, *Toronto, Ont.*	158	The Royal Montreal GC, Montreal, Que.
1905	George Cumming, *Toronto, Ont.*	148	P.F. Barrett, *Toronto, Ont.*	151	Toronto GC, Toronto, Ont.
1906	Charles Murray, *Montreal, Que.*	170	George Cumming, *Toronto, Ont.*	171	(Royal) Ottawa GC, Ottawa, Ont.
			*T.B. Reith, *Montreal, Que.*		
			Alex Robertson, *Victoria, B.C.*		
1907	Percy Barrett, *Toronto, Ont.*	306	George Cumming, *Toronto, Ont.*	308	Lambton G&CC, Toronto, Ont.
1908	Albert Murray, *Outremont, Que.*	300	George Sargent, *Ottawa, Ont.*	304	The Royal Montreal GC, Montreal, Que.
1909	Karl Keffer, *Toronto, Ont.*	309	George Cumming, *Toronto, Ont.*	312	Toronto GC, Toronto, Ont.
1910	Daniel Kenny, *Buffalo, NY*	303	*George S. Lyon, *Toronto, Ont.*	307	Lambton GC, Toronto, Ont.
1911	Charles Murray, *Montreal, Que.*	314	D.L. Black, *Rivermead, Ottawa, Ont.*	316	Royal Ottawa GC, Ottawa, Ont.
1912	George Sargent, *Washington, DC*	299	J.M. Barnes, *Tacoma, WA*	302	Rosedale GC, Toronto, Ont.
1913	Albert Murray, *Outremont, Que.*	295	Nicol Thompson, *Hamilton, Ont.*	301	The Royal Montreal GC, Montreal, Que.
			J. Burke, *Port Arthur, Ont.*		
1914	Karl Keffer, *Ottawa, Ont.*	300	George Cumming, *Toronto, Ont.*	301	Toronto GC, Toronto, Ont.
1915-18	NO TOURNAMENT				
1919	J. Douglas Edgar, *Atlanta, GA*	278	*R.T. Jones, *Atlanta, GA*	294	Hamilton G&CC, Hamilton, Ont.
			Karl Keffer, *Royal Ottawa*		
			J.M. Barnes, *St. Louis*		
1920 †	J. Douglas Edgar, *Atlanta, GA*	298	Charles Murray, *Montreal, Que.*	298	Rivermead GC, Ottawa Ont.
			*T.D. Armour, *Edinburgh, Scotland*		
1921	W.H. Trovinger, *Birmingham, MI*	293	Mike Brady, *Detroit, MI*	296	Toronto GC, Toronto, Ont.
			Bob Macdonald, *Chicago, IL*		
1922	Al Watrous, *Redford, MI*	303	Tom Kerrigan, *Siwanoy, NY*	304	Mt. Bruno GC, Montreal, Que.
1923	C.W. Hackney, *Atlantic City, NJ*	295	Tom Kerrigan, *Siwanoy, NY*	306	Lakeview GC, Toronto, Ont.
1924	Leo Diegel, *Washington, DC*	285	Gene Sarazen, *Briarcliff, NY*	287	Mt. Bruno GC, Montreal, Que.
1925	Leo Diegel, *Washington, DC*	295	Mike Brady, *Mamaroneck, NY*	297	Lambton GC, Toronto, Ont.
1926	MacDonald Smith, *Lakeville, L.I., NY*	283	Gene Sarazen, *New York*	286	The Royal Montreal GC, Montreal, Que.
1927	T.D. Armour, *Washington, DC*	288	MacDonald Smith, *Lakeville, L.I., NY*	289	Toronto GC, Toronto, Ont.
1928	Leo Diegel, *Mount Vernon, NY*	282	Archie Compston, *Great Britain*	284	Rosedale GC, Toronto, Ont.
			Walter Hagen, *New York*		
			MacDonald Smith, *Great Neck, L.I., NY*		
1929	Leo Diegel, *Agua Caliente, Mexico*	274	T.D. Armour, *Detroit, MI*	277	Kanawaki GC, Montreal, Que.
1930 †	T.D. Armour, *Detroit, MI*	277	Leo Diegel, *Agua Caliente, Mexico*	277	Hamilton G&CC, Hamilton, Ont.
1931 †	Walter Hagen, *Detroit, MI*	292	Percy Allis, *Germany*	292	Mississaugua G&CC, Mississauga, Ont.
1932	Harry Cooper, *Chicago, IL*	290	Al Watrous, *Birmingham, MI*	293	Ottawa Hunt Club, Ottawa, Ont.
1933	Joe Kirkwood, *Chicago, IL*	282	Harry Cooper, *Chicago, IL*	290	Royal York GC, Toronto, Ont.
			Lex Robson, *Toronto, Ont.*		
1934	T.D. Armour, *Chicago, IL*	287	Ky. Laffoon, *Denver, CO*	289	Lakeview GC, Toronto, Ont.
1935	Gene Kunes, *Norristown, PA*	280	Victor Ghezzi, *Deal, NJ*	282	Summerlea G&CC, Montreal, Que.
1936	Lawson Little, *Chicago, IL*	271	Jimmy Thomson, *Shawnee, PA*	279	St. Andrews GC, Toronto, Ont.
1937	Harry Cooper, *Chicopee, MA*	285	Ralph Guldahl, *Chicago, IL*	287	St. Andrews GC, Toronto, Ont.
1938 †	Sam Snead, *West Virginia*	277	Harry Cooper, *Chicopee, MA*	277	Mississaugua G&CC, Mississauga, Ont.
1939	Harold McSpaden, *Winchester, MA*	282	Ralph Guldahl, *Madison, NJ*	287	Riverside GC, Saint John, N.B.
1940 †	Sam Snead, *Shawnee-on-delaware, PA*	281	Harold McSpaden, *Winchester, MA*	281	Scarboro, G&CC, Toronto, Ont.
1941	Sam Snead, *Hot Springs, VA*	274	R.T. Gray, Jr., *Toronto, Ont.*	276	Lambton G&CC, Toronto, Ont.
1942	Craig Wood, *Mamaroneck, NY*	275	Mike Turnesa, *White Plains, NY*	279	Mississaugua G&CC, Mississauga, Ont.
1943-44	NO TOURNAMENT				
1945	Byron Nelson, *Toledo, OH*	280	Herman Barron, *White Plains, NY*	284	Thornhill GC, Toronto, Ont.
1946 †	George Fazio, *Los Angeles, CA*	278	Dick Metz, *Arkansas, KS*	278	Beaconsfield GC, Montreal, Que.
1947	Robert Locke, *South Africa*	268	Ed. Oliver, *Wilmington, DE*	270	Scarboro G&CC, Toronto, Ont.
1948	C.W. Congdon, *Tacoma, WA*	280	Dick Metz, *Virginia Beach, VA*	283	Shaughnessy Heights GC, Vancouver, B.C.
			Vic Ghezzi, *Englewood, NY*	283	
			Ky. Laffoon, *St. Andrews, IL*	283	
1949	E.J. "Dutch" Harrison, *Little Rock, AR*	271	Jim Ferrier, *San Francisco, CA*	275	St. George's G&CC, Toronto, Ont.
1950	Jim Ferrier, *San Francisco, CA*	271	Ted Kroll, *New Hartford, NY*	274	The Royal Montreal GC, Montreal, Que.
1951	Jim Ferrier, *San Francisco, CA*	273	Fred Hawkins, *El Paso, TX*	275	Mississaugua G&CC, Mississauga, Ont.
			Ed. Oliver, *Seattle, WA*	275	
1952	John Palmer, *Badin, NC*	263	Dick Mayer, *St. Petersburg, FL*	274	St. Charles CC, Winnipeg, Man.
			Fred Haas, Jr., *New Orleans, LA*	274	
1953	Dave Douglas, *Newark, DE*	273	Wally Ulrich, *St. Paul, MN*	274	Scarboro G&CC, Toronto, Ont.
1954	Pat Fletcher, *Saskatoon, Sask.*	280	Gordon Brydson, *Toronto, Ont.*	284	Point Grey G&CC, Vancouver, B.C.
			Bill Welch, *Kennewick, WA*	284	
1955	Arnold Palmer, *Latrobe, PA*	265	Jack Burke, Jr., *Kiamesha Lake, NY*	269	Weston G&CC, Toronto, Ont.
1956 †	*Doug Sanders, *Miami Beach, FL*	273	Dow Finsterwald, *Bedford Heights, OH*	273	Beaconsfield GC, Montreal, Que.
1957	George Bayer, *San Gabriel, CA*	271	Bo Wininger, *Odessa, TX*	273	Westmount G&CC, Kitchener, Ont.

YEAR	WINNER	SCORE	RUNNER-UP	SCORE	COURSE AND VENUE
1958	Wesley Ellis, Jr., *Ridgewood, NJ*	267	Jay Hebert, *Sanford, FL*	268	Mayfair G&CC, Edmonton, Alta.
1959	Doug Ford, *Paradise, FL*	276	Bo Wininger, *Odessa, TX*	278	Club de golf Islesmere, Montreal, Que.
			Dow Finsterwald, *Tequesta, FL*	278	
			Art Wall, Jr., *Pocono Manor, PA*	278	
1960	Art Wall, Jr., *Pocono Manor, PA*	269	Jay Hebert, *Lafayette, LA*	275	St. George's G&CC, Toronto, Ont.
			Bob Goalby, *Crystal River, FL*	275	
1961	Jacky Cupit, *Longview, TX*	270	Dow Finsterwald, *Tequesta, FL*	275	Niakwa CC, Winnipeg, Man.
			Buster Cupit, *Fort Smith, AR*	275	
			Bobby Nichols, *Midland, TX*	275	
1962	Ted Kroll, *Fort Lauderdale, FL*	278	Charles Sifford, *Los Angeles, CA*	280	Le Club Laval-sur-le-Lac, Montreal, Que.
1963	Doug Ford, *Tam O'Shanter, NY*	280	Al Geiberger, *Carlton Oaks, CA*	281	Scarboro G&CC, Toronto, Ont.
1964	Kel Nagle, *Sydney, Australia*	277	Arnold Palmer, *Laurel Valley, PA*	279	Pinegrove CC, St. Luc, Que.
1965	Gene Littler, *Las Vegas, NV*	273	Jack Nicklaus, *Columbus, OH*	274	Mississaugua G&CC, Mississauga, Ont.
1966	Don Massengale, *Jacksboro, TX*	280	Chi Chi Rodriguez, *Dorado Beach, Puerto Rico*	283	Shaughnessy G&CC, Vancouver, B.C.
1967 †	Bill Casper, *Peacock Gap, CA*	279	Art Wall, Jr., *Honesdale, PA*	279	Montreal Municipal GC, Montreal, Que.
1968	Bob Charles, *Christchurch, New Zealand*	274	Jack Nicklaus, *Columbus, OH*	276	St. George's G&CC, Toronto, Ont.
1969 †	Tommy Aaron, *Callaway Gardens, GA*	275	Sam Snead, *White Sulphur Springs, VA*	275	Pinegrove CC, St. Luc, Que.
1970	Kermit Zarley, *Houston, TX*	279	Gibby Gilbert, *Hollywood, FL*	282	London Hunt & CC, London, Ont.
1971 †	Lee Trevino, *El Paso, TX*	275	Art Wall, Jr., *Honesdale, PA*	275	Richelieu Valley GC, Ste-Julie de Vercheres, Que.
1972	Gay Brewer, Jr., *Dallas, TX*	275	Sam Adams, *Boone, NC*	276	Cherry Hill GC., Ridgeway, Ont.
			Dave Hill, *Jackson, MI*	276	
1973	Tom Weiskopf, *Columbus, OH*	278	Forrest Fezler, *Indian Wells, CA*	280	Richelieu Valley GC, Ste-Julie de Vercheres, Que.
1974	Bobby Nichols, *Akron, OH*	270	Larry Ziegler, *Terre Du Lac, MO*	274	Mississaugua G&CC, Mississauga, Ont.
			John Schlee, *Carrollton, TX*	274	
1975 †	Tom Weiskopf, *Columbus, OH*	274	Jack Nicklaus, *Muirfield Village, OH*	274	The Royal Montreal GC, Ile Bizard, Que.
1976	Jerry Pate, *Pensacola, FL*	267	Jack Nicklaus, *Muirfield Village, OH*	271	Essex G&CC, Windsor, Ont.
1977	Lee Trevino, *St. Teresa, NM*	280	Peter Oosterhuis, *Palm Springs, CA*	284	Glen Abbey GC, Oakville, Ont.
1978	Bruce Lietzke, *Beaumont, TX*	283	Pat McGowan, *Colusa, CA*	284	Glen Abbey GC, Oakville, Ont.
1979	Lee Trevino, *Dallas, TX*	281	Ben Crenshaw, *Austin, TX*	284	Glen Abbey GC, Oakville, Ont.
1980	Bob Gilder, *Corvallis, OR*	274	Leonard Thompson, *Orlando, FL*	276	The Royal Montreal GC, Ile Bizard, Que.
			Jerry Pate, *Pensacola, FL*	276	
1981	Peter Oosterhuis, *Santa Barbara, CA*	280	Bruce Lietzke, *Jay, OK*	281	Glen Abbey GC, Oakville, Ont.
			Andy North, *Madison, WI*	281	
			Jack Nicklaus, *North Palm Beach, FL*	281	
1982	Bruce Lietzke, *Afton, OK*	277	Hal Sutton, *Shreveport, LA*	279	Glen Abbey GC, Oakville, Ont.
1983 †	John Cook, *Rancho Mirage, CA*	277	Johnny Miller, *Mapleton, UT*	277	Glen Abbey GC, Oakville, Ont.
1984	Greg Norman, *Orlando, FL*	278	Jack Nicklaus, *Muirfield Village, OH*	280	Glen Abbey GC, Oakville, Ont.
1985	Curtis Strange, *Kingsmill, VA*	279	Jack Nicklaus, *Muirfield Village, OH*	281	Glen Abbey GC, Oakville, Ont.
			Greg Norman, *Orlando, FL*	281	
1986	Bob Murphy, *Stuart, FL*	280	Greg Norman, *Orlando, FL*	283	Glen Abbey GC. Oakville, Ont.
1987	Curtis Strange, *Kinsmill, VA*	276	David Frost, *Dallas, TX*	279	Glen Abbey GC. Oakville, Ont.
			Jodie Mudd, *Louisville, KY*	279	
			Nick Price, *Orlando, FL*	279	
1988	Ken Green, *Danbury, CT*	275	Bill Glasson, *San Diego, CA*	276	Glen Abbey GC. Oakville, Ont.
			Scott Verplank, *Edmond, OK*	276	
1989	Steve Jones, *Phoenix, AZ*	271	Mike Hulbert, *Orlando, FL*	273	Glen Abbey GC. Oakville, Ont.
			Mark Calcavecchia, *N. Palm Beach, FL*	273	
			Clark Burroughs, *Ponte Vedra Beach, FL*	273	
1990	Wayne Levi, *Newhartford, NY*	278	Ian Baker-Finch, *Queensland, Australia*	279	Glen Abbey GC. Oakville, Ont.
			Jim Woodward, *Oklahoma City, OK*	279	
1991	Nick Price, *Lake Mona, FL*	273	David Edwards, *Edmond, OK*	274	Glen Abbey GC, Oakville, Ont.
1992 †	*Greg Norman, *Orlando, FL*	280	Bruce Lietzke, *Dallas, TX*	280	Glen Abbey GC, Oakville, Ont.
1993	David Frost, *Dallas, TX*	279	Fred Couples, *S. Andros, Bahamas*	280	Glen Abbey GC, Oakville, Ont.

NAME CHANGED TO: BELL CANADIAN OPEN CHAMPIONSHIP

YEAR	WINNER	SCORE	RUNNER-UP	SCORE	COURSE AND VENUE
1994	Nick Price, *Lake Mona, FL*	275	Mark Calcavecchia, *W. Palm Beach, FL*	276	Glen Abbey GC, Oakville, Ont.
1995 †	*Mark O'Meara, *Windermere, FL*	274	Bob Lohr, *Orlando, FL*	274	Glen Abbey GC, Oakville, Ont.
1996	*Dudley Hart, *Ft. Lauderdale, FL*	202	David Duval, *Ponte Vedra Beach, FL*	203	Glen Abbey GC, Oakville, Ont.
	(event shortened to 54 holes due to weather)				
1997	Steve Jones, *Phoenix, AZ*	275	Greg Norman, *Hobe Sounde, FL*	276	The Royal Montreal GC, Ile Bizard, Que.
1998 †	*Billy Andrade, *Bristol, RI*	275	Bob Friend, *Pittsburgh, PA*	275	Glen Abbey GC, Oakville, Ont.
1999	Hal Sutton, *Shreveport, LA*	275	Dennis Paulson, *Encinitas, CA*	278	Glen Abbey GC, Oakville, Ontt.
2000	Tiger Woods, *Orlando, FL*	266	Grant Waite, *Palmerston North, New Zealand*	267	Glen Abbey GC, Oakville, Ont.
2001	Scott Verplank, *Edmond, OK*	266	Bob Estes, *Austin, TX*	269	The Royal Montreal GC, Ile Bizard, Que.
			Joey Sindelar, *Horseheads, NY*	273	
2002 †	John Rollins, *Richmond, VA*	272	Neal Lancaster, *Smithfielde, NC*	272	Angus Glen Golf Club, Markham Ont.
2003	Bob Tway, *Edmond, OK*	272	Brad Faxon, *Barrington, RI*	272	Hamilton G&CC, Ancaster, ON

* Denotes Amateur
† Denotes playoff (see page 219)

CANADIAN OPEN

MOST VICTORIES
4—Leo Diegel (1924, '25, '28, '29)
3—Tommy Armour (1927, '30, '34); Sam Snead (1938, '40, '41);
Lee Trevino (1971, '77, '79)
2—13 players

CONSECUTIVE VICTORIES
2—J. Douglas Edgar (1919, '20); Leo Diegel (1924, '25, 1928, '29);
Sam Snead (1940, '41); Jim Ferrier (1950, '51)

YOUNGEST CHAMPION
20 YEARS, 10 MONTHS, 2 DAYS—Albert Murray, 1908

OLDEST CHAMPION
44 YEARS, 4 MONTHS, 13 DAYS—Bob Tway, 2003

AMATEUR CHAMPIONS
Doug Sanders, Beaconsfield Golf Club, Pointe Claire, Que., 1956

LOW 72-HOLE SCORE BY AN AMATEUR
273—Doug Sanders, Beaconsfield Golf Club,
Pointe Claire, Que. 1956

CANADIAN CHAMPIONS
George Cumming, The Toronto GC, Toronto, Ont., 1905;
Charles Murray (2), Royal Ottawa GC, Aylmer, Que., 1906, 1911;
Percy Barrett, Lambton GC, Toronto, Ont., 1907;
Albert Murray (2), The Royal Montreal GC, Dixie, Que., 1908, 1913;
Karl Keffer (2), The Toronto GC, Toronto, Ont., 1909, 1914;
Pat Fletcher, Point Grey GC, Vancouver, B.C., 1954

RUNNER-UP FINISHES
7—Jack Nicklaus (1965, '68, '75, '76, '81, '84, '85)

TOP-TEN FINISHES
15—Charles Murray, 1904–1930
13—Jack Nicklaus, 1962–1995

LOWEST SCORE, 72 HOLES
263—Johnny Palmer (66-65-66-66), St. Charles Country Club,
Winnipeg, Man., 1952

MOST STROKES UNDER PAR, 72 HOLES
23—Johnny Palmer, St. Charles Country Club, Winnipeg, Man.,
1952

LOWEST SCORE, 18 HOLES
62 (10-under)—Greg Norman, third round, Glen Abbey Golf
Club, Oakville, Ont., 1986; (9-under) Leonard Thompson,
second round, Glen Abbey GC, Oakville, Ont., 1981; Andy Bean,
final round, Glen Abbey GC, Oakville, Ont., 1983

WINNING MARGIN
16 strokes—J. Douglas Edgar (278), Hamilton G&CC, Hamilton,
Ont., 1919

BEST FINISH BY A CHAMPION
63—Jerry Pate, Essex G&CC, LaSalle, Ont., 1976

HIGHEST WINNING SCORE
314—Charles Murray, Royal Ottawa GC, Alymer, Que., 1911

HIGHEST WINNING SCORE SINCE WORLD WAR II
283—Bruce Lietzke, Glen Abbey GC, Oakville, Ont., 1978

MOST PLAYERS TO MAKE CUT
83—Glen Abbey GC, Oakville, Ont., 1989

MOST CONSECUTIVE OPENS STARTED
22—Dan Halldorson, 1974-1995; Bruce Lietzke, 1975-1996

MOST OPENS STARTED
26—Dave Barr, 1976-2002

MOST OPENS COMPLETED 72 HOLES
23—Gordon Brydson, 1929–1956
22—Jack Nicklaus, 1962–1995

MOST CONSECUTIVE OPENS COMPLETED 72 HOLES
10—Mark McCumber, 1986-1995; Nick Price, 1986-1995

LONGEST SPAN, FIRST TO LAST VICTORY
8—Lee Trevino, 1971-79; Greg Norman, 1984-92; Steve Jones, 1989-97

LONGEST SPAN BETWEEN VICTORIES
8—Greg Norman, 1984-92; Steve Jones, 1989-97

LONGEST COURSE
7,372 yards—Angus Glen GC (The South Course), Markham, Ont., 2002

SHORTEST COURSE
5,125 yards—Toronto Golf Club, Toronto, Ont., 1905

SHORTEST COURSE SINCE WORLD WAR II
6,377 yards—St. Charles Country Club, Manitoba, 1952

SMALLEST FIELD
17 (1904)

PLAYOFFS (17)

1920 J. Douglas Edgar (73) def. Charles R. Murray (74) by one stroke and Tommy Armour (75) by two strokes in an 18-hole playoff.

1930 Tommy Armour (138) def. Leo Diegel (141) by three strokes in a 36-hole playoff.

1931 Walter Hagen (141) def. Percy Allis (142) by one stroke in 36-hole playoff.

1938 Sam Snead (67) tied Harry Cooper (67) in an 18-hole playoff. Snead defeated Cooper by five strokes in a nine-hole playoff.

1940 Sam Snead (71) def. Harold McSpaden (72) by one stroke in an 18-hole playoff.

1946 George Fazio (70) def. Dick Metz (71) by one stroke in an 18-hole playoff.

1956 Doug Sanders def. Dow Finsterwald with a par on the first playoff hole.

1967 Billy Casper (65) def. Art Wall (69) by four strokes in an 18-hole playoff.

1969 Tommy Aaron (70) def. Sam Snead (72) by two strokes in an 18-hole playoff

1971 Lee Trevino def. Art Wall with a birdie on the first playoff hole.

1975 Tom Weiskopf def. Jack Nicklaus with a birdie on the first playoff hole.

1983 John Cook def. Johnny Miller with a birdie on the sixth playoff hole.

1992 Greg Norman def. Bruce Lietzke with a par on the second playoff hole.

1995 Mark O'Meara def. Bob Lohr with a par on the first playoff hole.

1998 Billy Andrade def. Bob Friend with a par on the first playoff hole.

2002 John Rollins def. Neal Lancaster and Justin Leonard with a birdie on the first playoff hole.

2003 Bob Tway def. Brad Faxon with a bogey on the third playoff hole.

INDEX

A

Aaron, Tommy, 14, 59, 69, 188
Allis, Percy, 14
Alston, Rex, 113
American Society of Golf Course Architects, 76
Andrade, Billy, 22, 26, 158–159, 199
Angus Glen Golf Club, 28, 74, 77, 79, 83
architects (golf course). See designers
Armour, Tommy
    1920 Canadian Open, 54
    1924 Canadian Open, 77
    1927 Canadian Open, 45
    1929 Canadian Open, 57, 69
    1930 Canadian Open, 18, 95, 96–97
    as amateur in 1920, 164
    Canadian Open history, 11–12
    described, 10
    profile, 173
    Rivermead Challenge cup, 204
    three-time winner, 135, 164
Austin, Albert William, 71–72
Ayton, George, 54

B

Baker-Finch, Ian, 147
Balding, Al, 114, 114, 122, 165
Barclay, James, 113
Barnes, "Long" Jim, 8, 54, 75
Barr, Dave, 139, 145, 165
Barrett, Percy, 46, 58, 71, 72, 167
Barron, Herman, 15
Bayer, "Big" George, 124, 124, 183
Beaconsfield Golf Club, 16, 34, 57–58, 60, 63, 64
Bean, Andy, 8
Bell, Billy, 76
Bell Canada, 12, 205
Bell Canadian Open, 130, 205, 211
Bell Canadian Open Trophy, 205, 208
Bendelow, Tom, 55, 73, 75, 78, 80
Black, Davie, 54, 54

Bolt, "Terrible" Tommy, 19
Boros, Julius, 124
Brewer, Gay, 17, 20, 125, 190
Brisebois, Mario, 57
British Columbia, 107–111
the Bronfman family, 58
Bryant, Brad, 151
Brydson, Gordie, 16, 63, 103, 104

C

Calcavecchia, Mark, 26, 146, 152
Campbell, Tim, 119
Canadian Golfer, 51–54, 214
Canadian Open
    amateur win, 16
    Arnold Palmer, 18–19
    Bell Canadian Open, 130, 211
    Bobby "Muffin Face" Locke, 15–16
    Byron Nelson, 15
    Canadian winners, 7, 15, 16, 165
    18 putts record, 27
    entrance fees for spectators, 204
    72-hole record total, 119
    first decade of, 7
    first sudden-death playoff, 64
    first Sunday final round, 115
    first televised Open, 19, 21
    first tournament (1904), 7
    the Glen Abbey story, 22–23
    during Great Depression, 12
    Greg Norman, 24
    growth of, 6–7
    Hall of Fame decade, 12
    host clubs. See host clubs
    J. Douglas Edgar, 7–10
    Jack Nicklaus, 19–22
    Lee Trevino, 23–24
    left-handed winner, 115
    Leo Diegel, 10–11
    longest sudden-death playoff, 10, 139
    and the media, 213–215
    Nick Price, 26

    oldest champion, 165
    records, 218–219
    relaunching careers, 26
    Sam Snead, 12–14
    sponsors, 12
    Tiger Woods, 27–28
    Tommy Armour, 11–12
    triple or more winners, 135
    trophies, 203–208
    in 21st century, 28
    volunteers, 209–212
    winners and runners-up, list of, 216–217
    youngest champion, 23, 165
    youngest player to make cut, 16
Canadian Professional Golfers' Association Championship, 34
Carrick, Doug, 77, 79
Casper, Billy, 56, 58, 108, 187
CBC Radio, 213
Chapman, Dick, 93
Charles, Bob, 115, 119, 188
Cherry Hill Golf Club, 123, 124–125, 126, 127
Collinson, Jesse, 93
Colt, Harry, 7–8
Colt, H.S., 45, 48, 95, 99
Congdon, C.W. (Chuck), 107, 108, 179
Cook, John, 8, 10, 138, 164, 193
Cooke, Graham, 73
Cooper, "Lighthorse" Harry
    1932 Canadian Open, 51, 52
    1933 Canadian Open, 113
    1937 Canadian Open, 76
    1938 Canadian Open, 14, 52, 103
    profile, 174
    repeat winner, 164
    Riverside exhibition match, 92
Cornish, Geoffrey, 60
Couples, Fred, 151, 154
Crenshaw, Ben, 125
croquet style putting, 14
Cruickshank, Ian, 6, 71

Cumming, George
    1904 Canadian Open, 7
    1905 Canadian Open, 45, 46, 47
    Mississaugua Gold and Country Club, 105
    profile, 166
Cupit, Buster, 120
Cupit, Jacky, 120, *121*, 185

D

Daly, John, *42*, 137
designers
    A. W. Tillinghast, 16, 85, 89
    Albert Murray, 60
    A.V. Macan, 109
    David Gordon, 61
    Dick Wilson, 36
    Donald Ross. *See* Ross, Donald
    Doug Carrick, 77, 79
    Geoffrey Cornish, 60
    George Cumming, 105
    Herbert Strong, 77
    Howard Watson, 61
    H.S. Colt, 45, 48, 95, 99
    Jack Nicklaus, 129, 130, 131
    Kenneth Skodacek, 55
    Robert Trent Jones, 124, 126
    Stanley Thompson. *See* Thompson, Stanley
    Tom Bendelow, 55, 73, 75, 78, 80
    Walter J. Travis, 126
    William Gordon, 61
    Willie Dunn, 36, 73
    Willie Park, 55
    Willie Park, Jr., 60, 76–77, 79
Devlin, Bruce, 20, *116*
Diegel, Leo
    1920 Canadian Open, 54
    1924 Canadian Open, 58
    1925 Canadian Open, 72
    1928 Canadian Open, 75
    1929 Canadian Open, 69
    1930 Canadian Open, 18, 95, 96–97
    1933 Canadian Open, 113
    Canadian Open history, 10–11, 57
    four-time winner, 135, 164
    profile, 172
    Rivermead Challenge cup, 204
    World Golf Hall of Fame, 164
Douglas, Dave, 87–88, 181
Druid Hills Golf Club, 8
du Maurier, 12
du Maurier Trophy, 205, *207*
Dumfries and Galloway Club, 46
Dunlap, Scott, 156
Dunn, Willie, 36, 73
Duval, David, 27, 156

E

Edgar, J. Douglas
    1919 Canadian Open, 95
    1920 Canadian Open, 11, 51, 54
    Canadian Open history, 7–10
    mysterious death, 10
    profile, 170
    repeat winner, 164
    Rivermead Challenge cup, 204
Edwards, David, 26, 154
Ellis, Wes Jr., *119*, 120, 183
Essex Golf and Country Club, 123, 126

F

Faxon, Brad, 28, 97, 98, 165
Fazio, George, *64*, 178
Fazio, Tom, 64
Ferrier, Jim, 38, 101, 164, 180
Fezler, Forrest, 66
Finsterwald, Dow, 16, 64, 120
Fitzsimmons, Pat, 25
Fletcher, Pat
    1954 Canadian Open, 15, 16, 103, 108, 165
    profile, 181
Floyd, Raymond, 69
Forbes, Bruce, *130, 210*
Ford, Doug, 86, 88, 124, 164, 184
Freeman, Frank, *76*
Freeman, Willie, *76*
Friend, Bob, 22, 159
Frost, David, 26, 151, 197, 205

G

Geiberger, Al, 86, 88, 108
Ghezzi, Vic, 13
Gilbert, Gibby, 124
Gilder, Bob, *39*, 192
Glasson, Bill, 145
Glen Abbey Golf Club
    1984 Canadian Open, 24, 29
    1991 Canadian Open, 26
    1992 Canadian Open, 19
    1996 Canadian Open, 27
    "Big Chief," 20
    as Canadian Open host club, 128–161
    Cook-Miller sudden death finish, 10
    design by Nicklaus, 22–23
Goetz, Bob, 120
"Gold Dust Twins," 92
Golden Bear. *See* Nicklaus, Jack
Golf's Greatest (Goodner), 12
Goodman, Johnny, 58
Goodner, Ross, 12
Gordon, David, 61
Gordon, John, 75

Gordon, William, 61
Gray, Bob, 14, *63*, 86–87
greater-Montreal area Canadian Opens, 57–70
greater-Toronto area Canadian Opens, 75–83
    see also Toronto area Canadian Opens
Green, Ken, 144, 145, 149, 154, 195
Grimm, Richard, *130, 210*
Guldahl, Ralph, 86, 93

H

Hackney, Clarence W., 77, 171
Hagen, Walter
    1912 Canadian Open, 75
    1925 Canadian Open, 72
    1928 Canadian Open, 11
    1931 Canadian Open, 14
    charity exhibition matches, 93
    professional debut of, 76
    profile, 173
    Rivermead Challenge cup, 204
    in 1930s, 12
Hamilton, Gar, 103
Hamilton Golf and Country Club, 7–8, 18, 28, 54, 95–99
Harrison, Ernest Jerome "Dutch," 114, 179, 206
Hart, Dudley, 27, *156*, 198
Hebert, Jay, 120
Hewson, Karen, 45, 51
Hill, Dave, 108
Hogan, Ben, 93
Homenuik, Wilf, *65*, 66
host clubs (summary of Opens)
    see also specific host clubs
    Angus Glen Golf Club, 79
    Beaconsfield Golf Club, 60
    Cherry Hill Golf Club, 126
    Essex Golf and Country Club, 126
    Glen Abbey Golf Club, 131–133
    Hamilton Golf and Country Club, 99
    Islesmere (Club de Golf Islesmere), 60
    Kanawaki Golf Club, 60
    Lakeview Golf Club, 78
    Lambton Golf and Country Club, 73
    Laval-sur-le-Lac (Le Club Laval-sur-le-Lac), 61
    London Hunt and Country Club, 126
    Mayfair Gold and Country Club, 121
    Montreal Municipal Golf Club, 61
    Mount Bruno Golf Club, 60
    Niakwa Country Club, 121
    Ottawa Hunt Club, 55
    Pinegrove Country Club, 61
    Point Grey Golf and Country Club, 109
    Richelieu Valley Golf Club, 61
    Rivermead Golf Club, 55

Rosedale Golf Club, 78
The Royal Montreal Golf Club, 36
Royal Ottawa Golf Club, 55
Royal York/St. George's Golf & Country
    Club, 116
Scarboro Golf and Country Club, 89
Shaughnessy Golf and Country Club, 109
Shaughnessy Heights Golf Club, 109
St. Andrews Golf Club, 78
St. Charles Country Club, 121
Summerlea Golf and Country Club, 60
Thornhill Country Club, 79
Toronto Golf Club, 47
Westmount Golf and Country Club, 126
Weston Golf and Country Club, 79
Howell, Charles, 28
Huot, Jules, 57
Huot, Rudolphe, 93
the Huots, 57
Hurricane Fran, 156
Hutchinson, Jock, 54

I

Imperial Tobacco Company, 205, 210
Internet, 215
Islemere (Club de Golf Islesmere), 60

J

Jacobs, Tom, 120
Jenkins, Tom, 103
Jones, Bobby, 8, 54, 95–96, *96*, 164
Jones, Robert Trent, 124, 126
Jones, Steve
    1989 Canadian Open, 147
    1997 Canadian Open, 35
    gap between wins, 42, 149
    longest gap between victories, 164
    profile, 196
    relaunch of career, 26
    repeat winner, 164

K

Kanawaki Golf Club, 11, 60, 69
Keffer, Karl
    1914 Canadian Open, 15
    1919 Canadian Open, 8, 96
    Canadian-born winner, 7
    as Cumming protegé, 45
    profile, 168
    repeat winner, 45, 164
Kenny, Daniel, 72, 169
Kerr, Archie, 46–47
Kinnear, J.B., 54
Kirkwood, Joe, 113–114, 174
Knudson, George, 115, *115, 123*, 165

Kroll, Ted, 58, *66*, 185
Kunes, Gene, *62, 175*

L

Laird, Douglas, 46
Lakeview Golf Club, 11, 77, *77*, 78
Lambton Golf and Country Club, 11, 14,
    71–74, 86
Lancaster, Neal, 28, 83
Laval-sur-le-Lac (Le Club Laval-sur-le-Lac),
    58, 61, 65, 66
Lenzcyk, Grace, 93
Leonard, Justin, 83
Leonard, Stan, *63, 107*, 165
Levi, Wayne, *147*, 196
Lietzke, Bruce
    1978 Canadian Open, 130
    1982 Canadian Open, 135
    1992 Canadian Open, 19, 24, 149
    du Maurier Trophy, 205
    profile, 192
    repeat winner, 164
Little, Lawson, 76, 92, 175
Littler, Gene "The Machine," 20, 103, 186
Llittle, Lawson, 12
Lock, W.J., 75
Locke, Bobby "Muffin Face," 15–16, 85, 87, *88*,
    178
London Hunt and Country Club, 123, 124,
    126
longest sudden-death playoff, 10
"Lord" Byron. *See* Nelson, Byron
Love, Davis III, 143
low Canadian honours, 65
Lyon, George, 72, 73

M

Macan, A.V., 109
MacLaughlin, Bob, *213*
Mangrum, Lloyd, 107
Marshall, John, 210
Massengale, Don, 108, 109, 187
Mauch, Gene, 59
Mayfair Gold and Country Club, *118*, 119, *119*,
    120, 121
McGuire, Peter, 91
McIsaac, Rod, 126, *210*
McKay, Garry, 95
McSpaden, Harold "Jug"
    1939 Canadian Open, 14, 91, 92–93
    1940 Canadian Open, 86, 88
    1941 Canadian Open, 72
    charity exhibition matches, 93
    profile, 176
the media, 213–215

Medlen, Jeff "Squeeky," *154*
Metz, Dick, 64
Middlecoff, Cary, 107
Miller, Johnny, 8, 10, 138
Mississaugua Golf and Country Club, 14, 20,
    101–105
Montreal-area Canadian Opens, 33–44, 57–70
Montreal Municipal Golf Club, *56, 58*, 61
Morland, David IV, *43*
Mount Bruno Golf Club, 10, 57, *58*, 60
Murdoch, Allison, 93
Murphy, Bob, 143, 195
Murray, Albert
    as Cumming protegé, 45
    Kanawaki Golf Club designer, 60
    profile, 168
    repeat winner, 7, 164
    youngest champion, 23, 165
Murray, Charles
    1905 Canadian Open, 46
    1906 Canadian Open, 51, 57
    1911 Canadian Open, 51, 57
    as Cumming protegé, 45
    golf history, 23
    profile, 167
    repeat winner, 7, 164

N

Nagel, Kel, 69
Nagle, Kel, 98, 186
Nelford, Jim, 93, 129
Nelson, Byron
    1939 Canadian Open, 92
    1945 Canadian Open, 13, 76
    Canadian Open history, 15
    charity exhibition matches, 93
    profile, 177
    record of 113, 35
    Seagram Gold Cup, 205
Niakwa Country Club, 119, 120, 121
Nichols, Bobby, 103, 120, 191
Nicklaus, Jack
    1960 Canadian Open, 115
    1962 Canadian Open, 58
    1965 Canadian Open, 103
    1966 Canadian Open, 108
    1975 Canadian Open, 17, 33–34
    1976 Canadian Open, 38, 125–126
    1981 Canadian Open, 135
    1983 Canadian Open, 10
    1984 Canadian Open, 24, 29
    1986 Canadian Open, 143
    Canadian Golf Hall of Fame, 130
    Canadian Open history, 19–22
    Glen Abbey exhibition opener, 129

Glen Abbey Golf Club, 131
    against Strange, in 1985, 12
Norman, Greg "The Shark"
    1984 Canadian Open, 29, 139
    1985 Canadian Open, 22
    1986 Canadian Open, 143
    1992 Canadian Open, 19
    Canadian Open history, 24
    du Maurier Trophy, 205
    longest gap between victories, 164
    profile, 194
    relaunch of career, 26
    repeat winner, 164

O

O'Brien, Larry, 58
Oke, John H., 7, 7, 33, 46, 166
Oliver, Ed "Porky," 85, 87, 88
Olympic Games (1904), 72
O'Meara, Mark, 26, 198
Oosterhuis, Peter, 135, 193
Ottawa-area Canadian Opens, 51–56
Ottawa Hunt Club, 51, 52, 55
Ouimet, Frances, 95
owner-player disputes, 58–59

P

Palmer, Arnold
    1955 Canadian Open, 21, 76–77
    1964 Canadian Open, 69
    1965 Canadian Open, 20, 101
    1972 Canadian Open, 125
    Canadian Open history, 18–19
    first televised win, 215
    profile, 182
    Seagram Gold Cup, 205
Palmer, Johnny, 119, 120, 164, 180
Panasik, Bob, 16
Park, Willie, 55
Park, Willie Jr., 60, 76–77, 79
Pate, Jerry, 125, 126, 191
Pavin, Corey, 27
Perkins, Dave, 85
Peter Jackson Trophy, 205
PGA Tour
    owner-player disputes, 58–59
    Triple Crown, 11, 23–24, 59, 159, 165
Phillips, Randy, 33
Pinegrove Country Club, 14, 59, 61, 68, 69
Player, Gary, 65, 101
Point Grey Golf and Country Club, 15, 16, 108, 109
the Prairies, 118–121
Price, Nick
    1984 Canadian Open, 29, 139

1991 Canadian Open, 149, 154
1994 Canadian Open, 130, 152
Canadian Open history, 26
du Maurier Trophy, 205
Jeff Medlen, caddy of, 154
profile, 197
repeat winner, 164

R

radio coverage, 214
records, 218–219
Reith, Tom, 164
Richelieu Valley Golf Club, 11, 23, 59, 61, 67
Ritchie, Darren, 91, 93
Rivermead Challenge Cup, 203
Rivermead Golf Club, 8, 51, 52–53, 55, 204
Riverside Country Club, 14, 91–94
Rodriguez, Chi Chi, 58, 103, 108, 109
Rollins, John, 28, 77, 83, 201
Rosedale Golf Club, 11, 72, 75, 75, 78, 80
Ross, Donald
    and American Society of Golf Course
        Architects, 76
    Essex Golf and Country Club, 125, 126
    and Lambton Golf and Country Club, 73
    Riverside Country Club, 91, 93
    Rosedale Golf Club, 11, 78, 80
    St. Charles Country Club, 121, 126
Royal Canadian Golf Association, 6, 12, 204–205, 210
The Royal Montreal Golf Club
    1975 Canadian Open, 17, 20–22, 25
    1997 Canadian Open, 27
    as Canadian Open host club, 33–44
    first Canadian Open, 23
    first Open, 7
Royal Ottawa Golf Club, 7, 50, 51, 55, 57
Royal York Golf & Country Club, 112–117
Royal York/St. George's Golf & Country Club, 112–117
Rubenstein, Lorne, 129
Rudolph, Mason, 20
Ryder Cup, 26, 43, 93

S

Sanders, Doug, 16, 57–58, 64, 164, 182
Sarazen, Gene, 10, 57, 77, 93, 113
Sargent, George, 75, 169
Saskatchewan Golf and Country Club, 16
Scarboro Golf and Country Club, 14, 16, 85–89
Seagram, E. Frowde, 13
Seagram Company, 12, 114, 205
Seagram Gold Cup, 205, 206
Shaughnessy Golf and Country Club, 54, 108, 109, 110

Shaughnessy Heights Golf Club, 107, 109
Sifford, Charlie, 18, 58, 65, 66, 121
Silver Scot. See Armour, Tommy
Skodacek, Kenneth, 55
Slammin' Sammy. See Snead, Sam
Slater, Ray, 18–19
Smith, Alex, 75
Smith, Horton, 92
Smith, MacDonald, 172
Snead, Sam
    1938 Canadian Open, 52, 103
    1940 Canadian Open, 85–86
    1941 Canadian Open, 71, 72–73
    1969 Canadian Open, 59, 69
    Canadian Open history, 12–14
    charity exhibition matches, 93
    profile, 176
    Seagram Gold Cup, 205
    three-time winner, 135, 164
Somerville, Sandy, 124
southwestern Ontario, 123–127
St. Andrews Golf Club, 76, 77, 78
St. Charles Country Club, 119–120, 120, 121
St. George's Golf & Country Club, 112–117
St. George's Golf and Country Club, 76
Strange, Curtis, 12, 22, 129, 144, 164, 194
Stricker, Steve, 151
Strong, Herbert, 77
sudden-death playoff
    first, 64
    longest, 10, 139
Summerlea Golf and Country Club, 60, 62
Sutton, Hal, 26, 135, 199

T

Tait, 46
television coverage, 215
Tellier, Louis, 54
Thompson, Leonard, 135
Thompson, Stanley
    and American Society of Golf Course
        Architects, 76
    contributions of, 75–76
    Hutchinson, Ian, 101
    and Lambton Golf and Country Club, 73
    Mayfair Golf and Country Club, 121
    Mississaugua Golf and Country Club, 103, 105
    Niakwa Country Club, 121
    St. Andrews Golf Club, 76
    St. George's Golf and Country Club, 76, 113, 116
    Thornhill Country Club, 13, 76, 79
    Westmount Golf and Country Club, 124, 126
Thomson, Jimmy, 92
Thomson, Mabel, 92

Thomson, Percy W., 91–92
Thornhill Country Club, 13, 15, 76, 79, 82
Tillinghast, A.W., 16, 85, 89
Tolley, Cyril, 54
Toronto area Canadian Opens
  Glen Abbey Golf Club, 128–161
  greater-Toronto area clubs, 75–83
  Royal York/St. George's Golf & Country
    Club, 112–117
  Scarboro Golf and Country Club, 85–89
  Toronto Golf Club, 45–49
Toronto Golf Club, 7, 15, 45–49
TPD (Tournament Players Division) Tour, 59
Travinger, W.H., 45
Travis, Walter J., 126
Trevino, Lee
  1971 Canadian Open, 11, 59, 66
  1977 Canadian Open, 23–24
  1979 Canadian Open, 135
  du Maurier Trophy, 205
  profile, 189
  three-time winner, 164
  Triple Crown, 11, 165
Triple Crown, 11, 23–24, 59, 159, 165
trophies, 203–208
Trovinger, W.H., 170
Tryon, Ty, 16
Turnesa, Jim, 124
Tway, Bob, 28, 97, 99, 165, 201

U
Ulrich, Wally, 88
"umbrella" Open, 120
United States Golf Association, 14
V
Vardon, Harry, 72, 73
Verplank, Scott, 43, 145, 200
volunteers, 209–212

W
Waite, Grant, 27, 28, 160–161
Wall, Art Jr., 11, 23, 56, 66, 114, 184
Walzer, Winnie, 18, 19, 21
Warrington, Doug, 19
Warrington, Tom, 19
Watrous, Al (Andrew Albert), 58, 171
Watson, Howard, 61
Watson, Tom, 24
Weibring, D.A., 154
Weir, Mike, 28, 86, 91, 98, 165
Weiskopf, Tom
  1973 Canadian Open, 66
  1975 Canadian Open, 17, 17, 20, 33–34
  Canadian Open history, 38
  Glen Abbey exhibition opener, 129
  profile, 190
Welch, Bill, 16
Weslock, Nick, 93

Westmount Golf and Country Club, 16, 123,
  124, 125, 126
Weston Golf and Country Club, 18, 21,
  76–77, 79
Wilson, Dick, 36
Wood, Craig, 177
Wood, Fred, 63
Woods, Tiger, 40
  1996 Canadian Open, 156
  1997 Canadian Open, 35, 40
  2000 Canadian Open, 9, 130
  Canadian Open history, 27–28
  profile, 200
  Triple Crown, 59, 159, 165
Woodward, Jim, 147

Y
Young, Rick, 123
youngest player to make PGA cut, 16

Z
Zarley, Kermit, 124, 189, 205
Ziegler, Larry, 103, 103
Ziemer, Brad, 107
Zoeller, Fuzzy, 24
Zokol, Richard, 24, 29, 129, 143

ACKNOWLEDGEMENTS

This book could not have been compiled, in fact there would be little to write about, without the generosity of the sponsors of the Open; Seagram, Imperial Tobacco Ltd. and Bell Canada. Or the many volunteers, led by the volunteer chairman of the Open each year; Jim Clark, Ed Barnes, Rick Desrochers, Brad Turley, W. Keith Gray, Robert Long, John Dobson, Wm. Farlinger, R.H. Grimm, Cecil Vineburg, David H. Shea, J. A. Bailey, Albert Rolland, Peter J.G. Bentley, Patrick Osler, Ray Getliffe, Phil Farley, Ted McCall, Ken King, A Leroux among so many others. There have been a limited number of staff who could be named as pivotal to the success of the Open over an extended period of time. B.L. Anderson, Bill Taylor, Robbie Robinson, Paddy Kavanaugh, R. Bruce Forbes, Richard H. Grimm, Geordie Hilton, Stephen Ross, Bill Paul, Vera Clow, Ena Smith, Marion Doherty. The 2004 RCGA Board of Governors, and 2004 President David Shaw. Much of the work in compiling the book itself was done through the dedicated work of RCGA Staff; Paul Stone, Sarah Patten, Alison King, Victor Cui and Golf Canada Editor John Tenpenny. The Key Porter staff have been excellent, especially Michael Mouland, Peter Maher, Clare McKeon, and freelance designer Ingrid Paulson. We must not forget the many individuals who have played in the open since 1904, most of whom are listed on the end papers of the book, in an all time field list. There are some names missing—unfortunately not all fields were recorded in their entirety.

Tommy Aaron, Jerry Abbot, Bob Ackerman, Joe Acosta Jr., A.A. Adams, Adam Adams, Frank Adams, John Adams, Sam Adams, Ted Adams, Bob Adamson, Mitch Adcock,, Don Addingto...
Allin, Percy Allis, R. Allman, Stanton Altgelt, Robert M. Alston, Stephen Ames, Cy Anderberg, B.L. Anderson, Bud Anderson, C. Anderson, C.H. Anderson, Chris Anderson, E.L.H. And...
Appleby, Pierre Archambault, George Archer, J. Archer, K. Archibald, Jack Armitage, Tommy Armour, Tommy Armour III, Arthur Armstrong, Ty Armstrong, Wally Armstrong, Dewey A...
Baird, Butch Baird, Stan Baird, Doug Bajus, Bobby Baker, Cyril Baker, Ian Baker-Finch, Al Balding, John Baldwin, Seve Ballesteros, Ken Banks, Eric Bannister, Henry Barabin, Bob Ba...
Barrett, Jacques Barrette, Jerry Barrier, Doug Barron, Herman Barron, Chris Baryla, Rich Bassett, Bob Batdorff, Brian Bateman, Ben Bates, Pat Bates, Rey Batley, Eric Batten, Gary Bauer...
Begay III, Russell Beiersdorf, Joe Belfore, Brad Bell, Norman A. Bell, Willie J. Bell, Deane Beman, Mike Bender, Jim Benepe, Aaaron Bengoechea, Tony Benns, Ernie Bentley, Peter Bent...
Biancalana, L. Biddell, Don Bies, George F. Bigham, Carman Bill, Adrien Bigras, Jack Bissegger, Ben Bissell, Ted Bishop, David L. Black, Davie Black, Doug Black, G. Black, James A. Black...
A. Bloor, Elmer L. Blower, James D. Boeckh, Allan Boes, Steve Bogan, Scott Bogle, Marty Bohem, Bob Boldt, Rob Boldt, George Bolesta, Charles Bolling, Dave Bollman, Tommy Bolt, Pau...
Bourne, W. Bourne, Craig Bowden, Gary Bowerman, Charlie Bowles, Steve Bowman, Bob Boyd, T. Boyd, A. Boyer, William Boyle, W.W. Boyne, Frank Boynton, Michael Bradley, Mic...
Danny Briggs, Eldon Briggs, Luc Brien, Mike Bright, Mike Brisky, Bill Britton, Victor Brock, John Brodie, Steve Brodie, Ed Brook, Mark Brooks, G.P. Brophy, Al Brosch, Billy Ray Brown...
Bryant, Brad Bryant, Gordon Brydson, Jeff Buder, Jason Bucha, Howard Buchanan, Jace Bugg, Jason Buha, Bruce Bulina, Johnny Bulla, Jim Bullard, Jack Burk, William Burke, Jack B...
Jonathan Byrd, Curt Byrum, Tom Byrum, Angel Cabrera, George Cadle, Tom Cairns, Mark Calcavecchia, J. Caldwell, J.E. Caldwell, Rex Caldwell, Bill Calfee, Dan Cameron, Jack C. Came...
Joe Carr, A.C. Carrick, Donald D. Carrick, Jim Carter, Tom Carter, Billy Casper, R.C.H. Cassels, Mike Cassidy, Nick Cassini, Bruce Castator, Andre Cazes, Antonio Cerda, Ron Cerrudo, J...
Jack Chinery, Ashley Chinner, K.J. Choi, George Christ, Dave Christensen, A.J. Christie, Brian Christie, Jim Christie, Michael Christie, Pat Cici, Stewart Cink, Rocky Ciociolo, Brian Cla...
Cochran, Herman Coelho, Dave Cogdell, Jim Colbert, Ben Colk, Gene Coghill, Bobby Cole, Matt Cole, F. Coleman, J.W. Coleman, Gavin Coles, H.B. Collin, Bill Collins, Jock Collins, Ron C...
Graham Cooke, Carl Cooper, Lance Cooper, Harry Cooper, Pete Cooper, Vic Corbett, Frank Corrigan, Merv Costello, Jeff Coston, Kawika Cotner, L. Cotton, Chris Couch, Richard Cough...
W. Creavy, Emerson Creed, W. Creighton, Ben Crenshaw, Marshall Crichton, D.T. Croal, Richard Cromwell, J.R. Cronyn, Bobby Cruickshank, A.E. Cruttenden, Bruce Cudd, Jay Cudd, H...
Cupit, Jacky Cupit, Rod Curl, Mel Currier, Lee Curry, James Curti Jr., George S. Curtis, A. Cuthbert, David Cuthbert, Archie Dadian, Jess Daley, Joe Daley, Sam Dalley, Rick...
Marco Dawson, Jimmy Day, Glen Day, Jim Deal, Robert Dean, John Dear, Leon DeCaire, F. Decker, Bryan DeCorso, John Deforest, Claude Defour, C. De Breyne, Gordon De Laat, Davi...
Deverall, Roberto De Vicenzo, Bruce Devlin, Sal DiBuono, D.C. Dick, Gardner Dickinson, Bob Dickson, Chris Dickson, Terry Diehl, Leo Diegel, Mike Dietz, Terry Dill, Andy Dillard, Chris...
Dave Douglas, Bruce Douglass, Dale Douglass, John Dowdall, Jim Dowling, Allen Doyle, Norman Doyle, P. Doyle, Eddie Draper, Tom Draper, Jon Drewery, Ron Drimak, James Driscol, B...
David Duval, J. Dwyer, R.W. Eaks, J. East, S. Easterbrook, Bob Eastwood, J. Douglas Edgar, Frank Edmonds, David Edwards, Danny Edwards, Jerry Edwards, Joel Edwards, David Eger...
Wes Ellis Jr., Ken Ellsworth, Ernie Els, George Eluck, Cam Emerson, Billy Emmons, Bob Erickson, Randy Erskine, A. Espinosa, Don Essig III, Bob Estes, Jim Estes, Tom Eubank, Brice...
Fanning, Phil Farley, Johnny Farrell, Niclas Fasth, Gary Fawcett, Guy Fawcett, Brad Faxon, George Fazio, J. Fazsezke, David Feherty, Rick Fehr, Al Feldman, John Felus, Jack Ferenz, Ke...
Findlay, Dow Finsterwald, Ed Fiori, J.H. Firstbrook, W.H. Firstbrook, Todd Fischer, W. Fisher, Ron Fitch, Woody Fitzhugh, Pat Fitzsimons, R.W. Fitzsimons, John Flannery, Bob Flaro...
Doug Ford, J.H. Forrester, Anders Forsbrand, Dan Forsman, Erin Fostey, John Fought, Frank Fowler, W.C. Fownes Jr., W. Fox, John Fram, William A. Francis, Carlos Franco, Brent Frank...
Fryatt, Frank Fuhrer, Keiichiro Fukabori, F.J. Fulton, Ken Fulton, Fred Funk, Rod Funseth, Jim Funston, Ed Furgol, Marty Furgol, Jim Furyk, Bobby Gage, Andre Gagnier, Bob Gajda, J...
Damien Gauthier, Brian Gay, John Geersten, Al Geiberger, Brent Geiberger, John Gentile, Ernest George, Ray Getliffe, Victor Ghezzi, A.H. Gibson, Charlie Gibson, Jim Gibson, Kelly Gibso...
F.P. Glass, Bill Glasson, Tom Gleeton, Charles E. Glosby, Lawrence Glosser, Randy Glover, Bob Goalby, Dale Goehring, Bob Goetz, Dick Goetz, Nick Goetze, Matt Gogel, Matthew Goggi...
Retief Goosen, J.C. Goosie, Jack Gordon, Jason Gore, Bryan Gorman, R.J. Gormully, David Gossett, Steve Gotsche, Jeff Gove, Mike Gove, Dick Govern, Paul Gow, C.E.L. Gower, Paul Gov...
Green, Neil Green, R.H. Green, Bert Greene, Chris Greenwood, Bobby Greenwood, Brad Greer, Joe B. Greer, Otto Greiner,,C.B. Grier, Roy Grieve, W.M. Griffith, Ed Griffiths, Tony Gri...
Jay Haas, Jerry Haas, Don Hachey, Clarence Hackney, Dave Hackney, John Hadden, Norbett Haefner, Walter Hagen, Joe Hager, J. Hale Jr., Art Hall, Gary Hallberg, Dan Halldorson, Jim...
Eric Hanson, Jim Harberson, Chick Harbert, Jack Harden, A.A. Hargraft, Len Harman, Claude Harmon, Claude Harmon Jr., Paul Harney, Chandler Harper, Ian Harper, Sandy Harper...
Hawkins, J. Hay, Dale Hayes, J.P. Hayes, Mark Hayes, Ted Hayes, Don Headings, Clayton Heafner, Vance Heafner, J.P. Heaney, Jerry Heard, David Hearn, Tom Hearn, Skeeter Heath, Jay...
Hendrie, Dick Hendrickson, Nolan Henke, Allan Henning, Harold Henning, Brian Henninger, John Henrick, Paul Henrick, E.R.L. Henry-Anderson, Bunky Henry, J.J. Henry, Mark Hen...
Mike Hill, Ray Hill, Norman Himes, Jimmy Hines, Lon Hinkle, Larry Hinson, Babe Hiskey, Jim Hiskey, George Hixon, Gabriel Hjertstedt, Glen Hnatiuk, David Hobby, Stan Hobert, Fred H...
Michael Homa, Stan Homenuik, Ted Homenuik, Wilf Homenuik, Herb Hooper, Mark Hopkins, P.H. Horgan III, John Horne, Stanley Horne, Rudy Horvath, Al Hosick, Al Houghton, Th...
Hunter, Mac Hunter, Jules Huot,, Ray Huot,,Rolland Huot, Rudolphe Huot, Lyle Hurschman, George Husband, John Huston, A. Hutchinson, D. Hutchinson, Jock Hutchison, George Hut...
Irwin, Tripp Isenhour, Bill Israelson, Don Iverson, W. Jack, Tony Jacklin, David Jackson, John Jacobs, Ken Jacobs, Tommy Jacobs, Peter Jacobsen, Barry Jaeckel, C.C. James, Derek James,...
Johansson, Bernard Johnson, Bob Johnson, Chip Johnson, Doug Johnson, Eric Johnson, George Johnson, Howie Johnson, J. Johnson, Kevin Johnson, Mark Johnson, Ned Johnson, Richar...
Grier Jones, Kent Jones, Robert T. Jones, Roy Jones, Steve Jones, Tom Jones, Pete Jordan, Tom Joyce, Jeff Julian, Jose Jurado, Steve Jurgensen, W. Kaiser, Arthur Kam, Brian Kamm, Cra...
Keeling, Karl Keffer, Jim Keim, Herman Keiser, T.B. Keith, Kari Kekki, Bob Keller, Al Kelley, Bill Kelley, Ken Kelley, George Kelly, Jerry Kelly, Peter Kelly, Skip Kendall, Bill Kennedy, Joh...
Stan Ketler, R. Kiely, John Kilburn, Dave Killen, Karl Kimball, John Kindred, Claude King, Frank King, George King, Jim King, R.H. Kingston, J.B. Kinnear, Frank Kiraly, E. Kirks, Joe...
Haruyoshi Kobari, Gary Koch, E. Kocsis, Stan Kolar, Allan Kompass, Takaaki Kono, Brian Kontak, Mike Korich, J. Koval, John Koval, Bill Kozak, Greg Kraft, Mike Krak, Bill Kratzert...
Douglas Laird, W.T. Laird, Bob Lamb, Willie Lamb, Larry Lamberger, J.L. Lambie, Jean-Louis Lamarre, Steve Lamontagne, Tom Lamore, Neal Lancaster, Joe Land, Ralph Landrum, J...
Brian Laycock, Babe Lazane, Joe Leblanc, Douglas Lecuyer, Han Lee, Stan Lee, Gerald Lees, Ian Leggatt, Cobie Legrange, Tom Lehman, Ted Lehman, Tony Lema, Jeff Leonard, Justin L...
Jeff Lewis, John Lewis, K.C. Liao, Frank Lickliter, Steven Liebler, Bruce Lietzke, Irving Lightstone, Walter Lilly, W.J. Lindfield, Pat Lindsey, Garnet Lineker, Arthur Linfield, W.S. Linga...
Loftus, Bob Lohr, Charles Lombard, Hugh Logan, Ralph Lomeli, Peter Lonard, Michael Long, T. Longo, W.H. Loomis, Lyn Lott, Dick Lotz, John Lotz, Tim Loustalot, Davis Love Jr.,...
MacLean, Bob MacDonald, Willie MacFarlane, Dave Mackenzie, Redvers Mackenzie, R.A. Mackie, M.T. MacKirell, E.A. MacNutt, Dick Madsack, Andrew Magee, Jerry Magee, Jeff Magg...
Mangrum, Frank Mann, Dave Marad, Bill Markham, Gary Marlowe, Dave Marr, Graham Marsh, H. Marsh, Kerney Marsh, James B. Marshall, B.H. Martel, Henry Martell, Fred Marti, L...
H. Mason, Don Massengale, Rik Massengale, Jim Masserio, Richard Massey, Dick Mast, Craig Matthew, Duke Matthews, Len Mattiace, Davidson Matyczuk, Gary Maue, Bill Mawhinney...
Bob McCallister, Ben McCallum, Ronnie McCann, Scott McCarron, E.K. McCarthy, John McComish, Gary McCord, Larry McCrary, J.H. McCulloch, Mike McCullough, Mark McCumber...
Pat McGowan, T. McGrath, N.G. McGregor, Brian McGuigan, Paul McGuire, Harry McIlree, D. McKellar, Bob McKendrick, Buck McKendrick, Charles F. McKenna, E. McKenna, Dav...
McNulty, Mark McNulty, Bill McPartland, A.F. McPherson, Spike Mcroy, Harold McSpaden, Robert McWatt, W. McWilliams, Mike Mealia, Rocco Mediate, Scott Medlin, W.E. Mehlorn, C...
J.B. Mickles, L.G. Mickles Jr., Cary Middlecoff, Danny Mijovic, Ron Milanovich, Vincent Eldred, A.J. Miles, Eldridge Miles, Mike Miles, Art Millea, Allen Miller, Andy Miller, Brady Miller...
Moe, Ed Moehling, Brian Mogg, Bryce Molder, Florentino Molina, Tony Mollica, H.C. Monk, L.A. Molner, John Monroe, Jack Montgomery, Eric Monti, Ron Montressor, Griff Moody, C...
IV, Mike Morley, A. Morris, D.D. Morrison, R.G. Morrison, T. Morrison, Tommy Morrow, John Morse, E.S. Moss, F.G. Moss, Perry Moss, Jerry Mowlds, Larry Mowry, Jodie Mudd, Mic...
Murray, K.C. Murray, Kelly Murray, Larry Nabholtz, Jack Nadash, W.E. Nagel, Kel Nagle, Bill Nary, Jack Nash, Ted Neist, Jim Nelford, Byron Nelson, Larry Nelson, Dwight Nevil, W...
Nielsen, Tom Nieporte, Charles Nixon, J.R. Nixon, Frank Nobilo, Dave Noble, Jess Noble, Joe Noble, Keith Nolan, Augie Nordone, Greg Norman, Moe Norman, Ben Norris, Tim Norri...
Lawrence O'Hearn, Aki Ohmachi, Jack O'Keefe, Jack Oke, John H. Oke, David O'Kelly, Paul O'Leary, C.C. Oliver, Ed Oliver, Doug Olson, Greg Olson, Peter Olynyk, Peter O'Malley, Mark...
Chuck Palmer, Johnny Palmer, L.A. Palmer, Rod Pampling, Bob Panasik, Bobby Pancratz, Brendan Pappas, Deane Pappas, Mike Parco, E. Parent, Bill Parker, F.A. Parker, Keith Parker, Pe...
Paulson, James Paulson, Corey Pavin, Bob Payne, George Payton, Eddie Pearce, Rick Pearson, Ted Pease, Mike Peck, Dave Peege, Calvin Peete, John Peirson, Bill Pelham, David Pember...
Perry, Kenny Perry, Scott Petersen, Les Peterson, Randy Petri, Tim Petrovic, Joe Pezzullo, Mark Pfeil, E.J. Pfister, H.W. Phelan, Robbie Phillips, Jimmy Picard, Harry Pidduck, Greg Pidlask...
Lee Porter, Johnny Pott, Joe Poulin, Jimmy Powell, Greg Powers, Bob Pratt, Jerry Preuss, Nick Price, Jerry Priddy, Dicky Pride, J. Pringle, Jack Pritchard, Bob Proben, Art Proctor, Gerry J...
Ralston, Ross Randall, John Randle, Sam Randolph, Henry Ransom, Joey Rassett, Charles Raulerson, Dick Rautmann, Lee Raymond, Milton Reach Jr., Mike Reasor, J. Redpath, Buster Re...
Rick Rhoads, Ted Rhodes, Dick Rhyan, Tad Rhyan, Gordon Richards, K.G. Richards, Ray Richer, F. Rickwood, T.A. Riddell, Skee Riegel, John Riegger, Jim Riggins, A. Riley, Chris Riley,...
James Robertson, John Robertson, W. Robertson, Phil Robeson, Bill Robinson, J.B. Robinson, R.F. Robinson, Lex Robson, Luc Rochefort, Phil Rodgers, Anthony Rodriguez, Chi Chi Rodri...
Rousseau, C.H. Rowe, Earl Rowley, Doug Roxburgh, Jimmy Roy, Hugh Royer, Hugh Royer III, Ed Rubis, Craig Rudolph, Mason Rudolph, John Ruedi, Jack Rule Jr., Dave Rummells, Pa...
Sander, Doug Sanders, Gary Sanders, Jeff Sanders, Monte Sanders,Tom Sanderson, R. Sansone, Cesar Sanudo, Gene Sarazen, George Sargent, Gene Sauers, Lanny Sawchuck, Ken Schall...
Eddie Schwartz, Brent Schwarzrock, Adam Scott, Norman M. Scott, Richard Scott, Steve Scott, Larry Sears, David Seawall, John Senden, N. Senior, Gib Sellers, Ed Selser, Kevin Senecal...
Short, George Shortridge, George Shoux, V. Shreeve, Densmore Shute, Tom Sieckmann, R. Curt Siegel, Charles Sifford, Curtis Sifford, Dan Sikes, R.H. Sikes, Tony Sills, Larry Silveira...
Skinner, Sonny Skinner, Gary Slatter, H. Slattery, Mark Slawter, Heath Slocum, Jeff Sluman, Mike Small, A.B. Smillie, Alex Smith, Bob E. Smith, Chris Smith, Don Smith, George Smith,...
Walter Smithers, J.C. Snead, Sam Snead, Ed Sneed, Terry Snodgrass, Ansel Snow, Bill Snow, Mick Soli, C. Ross Somerville, H. Somerville, August Sordone, Finn Sorense, Mike Souchak...
Springer, Mike Springer, F. Sprogell, Lefty Stackhouse, Craig Stadler, Mike Standly, Paul Stankowski, Bob Stanton, J.O. Stark, Nathaniel Starks, Larry Startzel, Kenneth Staton, F.T. Stau...
Stiles, Ken Still, Adrian Stills, Charles Stock, Dave Stockton, Dave Stockton Jr., Waddy Stokes, Bob Stone, Tom Storey, Ward Stouffer, Dick Stranahan, Frank Stranahan, Curtis Strange, F...
Sullivan, Brad Sutterfield, David Sutherland, Don Sutherland, Kevin Sutherland, W.M. Sutherland, Alex Sutton, Hal Sutton, Dan Swanson, Jim Swarbrick, Bill Swartz, Mike Swartz, Tim...
B. Taylor, H.T. Taylor, Harry Taylor, J. Percy Taylor, Glenn Teal, L. Tellier, Lance Ten Broeck, Brian Tennyson, David Tentis, Peter Teravainen, Jim Terry, Joe Tesori, Bert Tew, R.H. Tew...
Leonard Thompson, Nicol Thompson Jr., Nicol Thompson Sr., Rocky Thompson, R.O. Thompson, Robert Thompson, Stanley Thompson, W.F. Thompson, W.J. Thompson, W.G. Thom...
Tiziani, Mario Tiziani, Harry Todd, Rick Todd, John Toepel, Esteban Toledo, Tommy Tolles, David Toms, F.J. Torza, Harry Toscano, Bob Toski, Vaughan Trapp, John Traub, William G. T...
Tucker, Lloyd Tucker, Murray Tucker, Mike Turneau, Dick Turner, Ted Turner, Jim Turnesa, Joe Turnesa, Mike Turnesa, G.H. Turpin, Billy Tuten, Bob Tway, Greg Twiggs, Howard Twi...
Jim Veno, Scott Verplank, Bob Verwey, Stew Vickers, Ellsworth Vines, Everett Vinzant, Wayne Vollmer, George Von Elm, Ernie Vossler, Bobby Wadkins, Lanny Wadkins, Lloyd Wadkins, J...
Jackson Walton, Bobby Walzel, Fred Wampler, Bud Ward, Doug Warner, Charles Warren, Ken Wasslen, Randy Watkins, Scott Watkins, Nick Watney, Al Watrous, A. Watson, Denis Watson...
Weiskopf, Bill Welch, John Wells, Kevin Wentworth, Nick Weslock, Roger Wessels, Harold West, Mike West, Wayne Westner, David Wettlaufer, Ward Wettlaufer, Brett Wetterich, Dan Wha...
Roy G. Widstrom, Mark Wiebe, Jim Wiechers, Terry Wilcox, Earl Wilde, Frank E. Willey, F.C. Williams, Bill Williamson, Jay Williamson, Garrett Willis, A. Wilson, Alec Wilson, Brian Wil...
Fred J. Wood, L.E. Wood, Larry Wood, W.G. Wood, Wendell Wood, Willie Wood, Jeff Woodland, Eric Woods, Tiger Woods, A.B. Woodward, Jim Woodward, Len Woodward, Curtis Worde...
Kaname Yokoo, H.A. Yorke, J. Young, Kim Young, N. Young, Nelson Young, Wayne Young, Kenneth L. Yount, J.W. Yuile, Kas Zabowski, Bruce Zabriski, Joe Zakarian T...